RICHARD CHARKIN

Since becoming a publisher in 1972,
Richard Charkin has held many senior
posts at major publishing houses, including
Oxford University Press, Reed Elsevier,
Current Science Group, Macmillan, and
Bloomsbury Publishing. He is former
President of The Book Society, the
International Publishers Association and
the UK Publishers Association. He is a
non-executive director of the International
Advisory Board of the Frankfurt Book Fair,
Liverpool University Press, and Cricket
Properties Ltd as well as advising
nkoda.com and running Mensch
Publishing. He lectures on the
publishing courses at London College of
Communications, City University, and
University College London.

TOM CAMPBELL

Tom Campbell is an independent
consultant and writer. He has worked with
the Greater London Authority to produce
the Mayor's Cultural Strategy and was
Head of Creative Industries at the London
Development Agency. He co-chaired the
Creative Industries Council's Working
Group on Regions and Clusters and is on
the editorial board of the academic journal
Cultural Trends. His most recent novel,
The Planner, is published by Bloomsbury.

MY BACK PAGES

AN UNDENIABLY PERSONAL
HISTORY OF PUBLISHING:
1972-2022

MY BACK PAGES

AN UNDENIABLY PERSONAL HISTORY OF PUBLISHING: 1972-2022

RICHARD CHARKIN
with
TOM CAMPBELL

Marble Hill London

MY BACK PAGES

First published by Marble Hill Publishers in 2023

Flat 58 Macready House
75 Crawford Street
London W1H 5LP
www.marblehillpublishers.co.uk

A CIP catalogue record for this book is available from the British Library.

ISBN: 978-1-7392657-3-1
E-book ISBN: 978-1-7392657-4-8

Text and jacket design by Paul Harpin
Printed and bound by Ingram Spark

TABLE OF CONTENTS

TABLE OF CONTENTS

PREAMBLE

The last fifty years have arguably seen more change in the publishing industry than in the previous five hundred, and I was fortunate enough to have been there to see much of it. In working on this project, which was first suggested to me by an overgenerous lecturer leading a group of students on a publishing course, I have tried to paint an analogue picture of fifty years in the publishing industry. I wanted to highlight the massive changes: the significance of certain decisions, impacts of technology, the role of bodies and the actions of certain people.

Many people have worked in publishing for their entire working lives, and so I am hardly unusual in that regard. But if there has been anything distinctive about my career, then it is in the range of things I have done and seen, and people I have worked with. It is probably a reflection on my failings to ever properly have had a career plan, but at some point in the last fifty years I have worked across almost every kind of publishing there is: trade, fiction and non-fiction, academic and scientific, journals, medical textbooks, children's literature, education, dictionaries and reference. In the course of this I have worked for and with venerable institutions, family businesses, publicly listed companies and start-ups. I have faced wave after wave of over-hyped technology, and also genuine, transformative innovations and travelled the world meeting and dealing with brilliant publishers. And in every place I have worked, and every job I have had, there has been something that excited me and which I loved.

I wanted to make this as impersonal as possible – more about events than about me. I have failed through no fault of my diligent collaborator, Tom Campbell, and through no lack of effort on my part. Rather, because it has simply been too difficult to separate my career from what has been happening in the industry. If I attempted to be entirely objective then the project would swell, as so many publishing histories have, to an enormous length and take longer than the years I have left to complete. So here it is, warts (and there are many) and all, in the hope that there might at least be one or two lessons of value to current and future publishers or even to business historians who can hopefully enjoy the attempts of an amateur chronicler.

CHAPTER ONE: STARTING OUT

A publishing house in early 1970s Britain; the working life of a young editor; editing by candlelight; the 'gentleman publisher'; the advantages of hands-off management; beer and snooker; fast forward half a century; the modern office.

In January 1972 I started my first job in publishing at the offices of George G. Harrap, 182-4 High Holborn, five minutes' walk from the British Museum. I can't remember whether I had bought any new items of clothing for my first day at work, but I would have worn a dark suit and tie and black

Richard Charkin in 1972

leather shoes, the standard office wear for men. Unlike those working in the City of London or the civil service, there was no need for a bowler hat, but other than that I was dressed much the same. Only six months out of university and this being the early 1970s my hair was down to my collar with an element of 'Jewfro', but this was by no means unusual.

I was living in a cockroach-infested basement flat in South Kensington, now worth a small fortune, from where I got the Piccadilly line to the office. It was the year of Bloody Sunday, debilitating strikes by dockers and miners and persistently high inflation. The pound was about to touch $2.65 against the dollar (on the back of North Sea Oil hopes) and has never been as high since. Prime Minister Edward Heath was in the middle of negotiations to enable the UK to join the European Economic Community.

In the world of publishing, Agatha Christie's penultimate novel to feature Hercule Poirot was about to come out, and John Berger shared

1

half of his proceeds from winning the Booker Prize with the Black Panthers. But by far the biggest hit that year would be Richard Adams's *Watership Down*. As is often the way with these things, it had a curious publishing history – it had been published by Rex Collings, a former editor at Oxford University Press, who had set up his own firm focused on African literature. Adams had been turned down by all the major publishers before a friend passed it to Collings who for some reason decided to take a chance on a debut novel about talking rabbits, some of whom had telepathic powers. The book was such an enormous success that Collings, unable to fund the upfront costs of multiple reprints, sold the rights on to Penguin, allowing him to enjoy the rest of his career publishing African poetry and literature, bringing to Europe works by major writers such as Nobel laureate Wole Soyinka.

Elsewhere, President Nixon was about to embark on his state visit to the People's Republic of China while in the summer the video games company Atari was founded and the first working email network tested. Later that year, pocket calculators would go on sale in Britain. But these were the merest inklings of a world to come, and when I got to the office in 1972 it looked little different from any publishing house a century earlier.

On my first day, as with every subsequent day, I was admitted through the back door as the front entrance was reserved for authors and directors. Once inside, Harrap's offices occupied five storeys of a confusing and higgledy-piggledy building, with a layout seemingly based on its original construction. There was a treacherous goods lift and most people preferred to use the rickety staircase, with its steps covered in a durable material, now rarely seen, known as 'battleship linoleum'. For the first few weeks at least, I would get lost most days. The walls were yellow with a century of cigarette smoke and almost every one of the eighty or so members of staff, me included, cheerfully smoked while at work. The building was entirely rebuilt in the 1980s and has been the home of Arab Press House while the offices next door are those of Thames & Hudson and not too far away are Faber, Bloomsbury, Bonnier and several others, so it has very much remained part of a publishing district.

Much of the ground floor was taken up by the warehouse where printers delivered stock and where almost all the books were stored and distributed from. Running along the side of this was the trade counter. Much like at a builders' merchants, booksellers would walk in directly

2

without need of an appointment, order their books and have them handed to them there and then, or else delivered later that day, at a wholesale price of around 30% discount for 'net' (general) books and 17.5% for 'non-net' (educational). The counter was manned by one of the warehouse team who, cigarette permanently in his mouth, would write out the invoices by hand and make duplicate carbon copies.

The beating heart of the company was the copyediting team, who dominated the first floor. This was a pool of approximately ten people, some (to my eyes at least) elderly men and also one or two younger women, who sat together, had lunch together and went to the pub together. The senior copyeditor, Brian Graham, was regarded as the one truly indispensable member of the entire company. His chair was permanently positioned on a raised plinth so that he was better able to observe and keep an eye on his junior colleagues, and to reflect his higher status in the organisation. Whilst Brian was undoubtedly the boss, the most experienced copy editor was Roy Minton, whose father had worked at Harrap for fifty years. Sadly, Roy only managed 49 years there before being laid off, thus depriving his family of a well-earned century of dedication to the firm.

The notion of the open plan office in the modern sense didn't exist. Rather, I shared a converted attic at the top of the building with a couple of other editors and an assistant. I did have a telephone, or at least the room had one, but we were expected to keep calls to a minimum. If possible, you were encouraged to use the phone in the afternoon when there was a cheaper rate, while international calls were almost unheard of, and certainly never made by me. I did have a typewriter at home but I couldn't actually type. Indeed, it would have been notable if I had been able to, and none of my editor colleagues were proficient with one. I had handwritten all my essays while at university and never used a typewriter in earnest. Instead, I had a typist – or rather access to a typing pool. This was of a similar size to the copyediting team, but staffed entirely by women. I would write out letters and memos in longhand or dictate to one of the assistants. These would be typed out, almost always within the hour.

As with an editor today, much of my time was spent in correspondence with authors, and this was largely done by post. I had been there for some weeks before a senior manager took me to task for not being on top of the job. I hadn't realised that Harrap used a pigeonhole system and that, rather than being brought to my desk, all my mail was piling up in my hole in the post room. I should have known better: after all, it was exactly the same system that my college at Cambridge had been using for the last three hundred years. There was no photocopier – if there were to be multiple recipients, then letters had to be carbon copied and distributed to colleagues around the building. Of course, one of the great blessings of this, only belatedly realised many years later in the era of email, was that copies were kept to a minimum – the incessant copying in of managers, the convention of keeping everyone in the loop and getting feedback from team members was something that came much later. With making copies being so time consuming, it was only done when actually necessary.

The Victorian atmosphere at Harrap was heightened when, during my second year of working there, the three-day week was imposed. Taking place during the winter of 1973-74, this was the desperate attempt by Edward Heath's government to limit the use of electricity in the face of industrial action by coal miners. All 'non-essential' businesses were restricted to three days of energy consumption per week – and Harrap was unfortunately, if understandably, not deemed to be essential. It was a strange, but not necessarily unpleasant period, when we used candles in the office, buildings were unlit at night, and the national speed limit was reduced to 55 mph.

THE WORKING LIFE OF A YOUNG EDITOR

I had been hired as Assistant Science Editor, as far as I could tell, purely on the basis that I had a science degree, and was young and thus in-expensive. There was no internship, no requirement for a diploma or post-graduate study, nor indeed any experience of the publishing industry. I hadn't even worked in a bookshop. Nor was there any family history or connection to publishing, which has always been a traditional route into the industry. Until January 1972, the closest I had been to publishing was a student summer job in the post room of Haymarket Magazines which I had only managed to hold down for a few weeks before being sacked by Michael Heseltine for having had what he regarded as an overly friendly conversation with his wife.

In joining Harrap, I was able to become a member of the National Union of Journalists, an essential for my first career choice of becoming a journalist. This had been a primary motivation behind taking the job in the first place and by the end of my time there I was 'Father of the Chapel' – the senior shop steward of our union branch. Almost all of my colleagues were similarly trade union members. We had frequent union meetings, usually in the pub, and regular visits from a union convenor, a paid officer who advised on negotiations and disputes. It was an era of high inflation and government-mandated wage restraint, and so conversations between union representatives and management were a common and ongoing feature of most companies at the time.

Assistant Editor

Young Scientific Assistant Editor required to process London publisher's science and mathematics list. Must be capable of editing MSS to a high standard and of dealing with authors and proofs with the minimum of supervision. Salary £1200–£1500 p.a. Please apply to Ron Hawkins at Harrap, 405 9935.

The advert in the Bookseller which started it all

It had been a senior editor, Ron Hawkins, who had interviewed me and given me the job. There was no HR or Personnel department that I was ever aware of, and support services in general were minimal – no IT team obviously, but also very limited accounts, finance, facilities or legal officers. There was no finance director on the board and the role of the chief financial officer, the key figure in a modern company alongside the chief executive, did not really exist in Harrap or elsewhere in publishing at the time. In fact, there wasn't even really a chief executive. Paull Harrap (always referred to as Mr Paull, and curiously spelt with two Ls) was the nearest thing but there were other, possibly more powerful, characters in the background, about whom we knew very little. In fact, it wasn't even clear to me whether there was a Board. There was no marketing department and nor was there at any publishing company that I was aware of. There were two sales teams (schools and bookshops) and a small number of publicists, who produced catalogues and undertook a small amount of trade advertising. The notion of a marketing strategy was unimaginable.

My starting salary at Harrap was £1200 a year plus luncheon vouchers, which would allow me to buy a Spanish omelette sandwich from the café round the corner. Employers could give their staff vouchers worth up to three shillings (or 15p post-decimalisation) every day, five days a week tax free. The average British male salary in 1972 was just under £2000 a year, and £1100 for a female, so for a first job out of university, it was by no means badly paid, although lower than today's starting salaries allowing for inflation. It certainly felt like a reasonable amount of money and enough to go out in the evenings to socialise. The fundamental difference was the London property market. On this kind of salary and before the invention of student debt, I could afford to rent a room in central London without moving back with my mother.

From the perspective of 2022, perhaps the most surprising thing about my employment package was that I was given a car – a Morris Marina, possibly one of the worst cars ever made by British Leyland. Just as surprising is that I would sometimes use it to drive to work, and would park round the corner from the office in the centre of London. Other than that, I had very little need for it. But the 1970s was very much the age of the company car and, at a time of high rates of income tax, it was a common employment perk. Apart from the occasional visit to an author, I actually had little need for a car and, as tended to happen, once I married my wife would use it far more than I ever did.

Although he hadn't interviewed me, my 'line manager' (a phrase which probably didn't exist then) was Patrick Heyworth who was in charge of the education side. Heyworth favoured a hands-off approach to management and was frequently to be found at the Garrick Club. On special occasions he would treat his young editors there and always insist that we piled into a taxi, even though it was no more than a short walk. He didn't take much interest in the business, but he at least tried to make sure our salaries kept pace with inflation, enjoyed a comfortable lifestyle and retired to the south of France as soon as he was able.

Heyworth never really told me what, for the purposes of my role, constituted science – biology, chemistry, physics, engineering and maths were all included. It was vaguely understood, but never specified, that science would also cover medicine. Nor was the market or sector segmented in any way: my remit covered the general reader (popular science wasn't a term used then), schools, universities and anything else that came in between. I was a 22-year-old allowed to pretty much blunder around, publishing anything related to science that I thought could make money. It was science publishing, but hardly scientific.

It did mean that there were opportunities for a young editor to use his initiative. I had been there a few months when we were sent two volumes from an American publisher of Isaac Asimov's dictionaries, *Words of Science* and *More Words of Science*. I licensed the UK rights, but thought it would work better integrated into a single volume. Roy Minton did the production, we reset the text and published it as simply *Words of Science*. However, when it came to pricing, the costs were such that on a 5000-print run we would have had to charge too high a price or else lose money. I met with a former colleague, Mike O'Mara, who had just moved to the Book Club Associates, and he suggested that we should print 15,000 copies to make the numbers work. He ordered 10,000 copies for the BCA (it would be the first of many times that the BCA would prove to be a saviour for me) and the book became a staple of many 1970s family homes.

My editorial colleagues at Harrap seemed to have similarly broad roles. Probably the most successful editor while I was there was Joe Gaute who, among other things, oversaw a list of true crime titles. In 1974 he published the autobiography of Albert Pierrepoint, Britain's most prolific hangman, responsible for executing several hundred people over three decades. Not surprisingly, it was a huge seller. Equally popular, and far more wholesome, was the Milly-Molly-Mandy series of children's books written and illustrated by Joyce Lankester Brisley. Originally printed in the Christian Science Monitor before the war, these genteel tales of a little girl in a pink and white dress growing up near the English seaside were still going strong in the 1970s. When, as tended to happen, company revenues were failing to keep up with expectations the remedy was invariably to come up with a new format for M-M-M. Decades later, I would see the same strategy being applied for the Gruffalo and Harry Potter.

When people look back on the 1970s, they often tend to think that publishing, much like Fleet Street newspapers, had a 'drinking culture'. It's certainly the case that almost all of us went to the pub at lunchtime and would drink a couple or more pints of beer. The local favourite was the Princess Louise, a classic Victorian London pub still going strong to this day. Back then, it had separate public and lounge bars. The dozen or so warehouse workers always went to the public bar, while the editorial and management went to the lounge – an unspoken rule that we all rigidly followed. There was also a nearby underground snooker club (forbidden to women) where you could also get a drink and which was popular among staff in the evenings, or even at lunchtime or the afternoon if things were quiet.

So it was normal to drink at lunchtime, and everyone smoked. But none of this was especially decadent – expensive lunches, long sessions in wine bars with authors and extravagant book launches weren't something I encountered until the late 1980s. People may have drunk beer with their lunch and gone out in the evenings during the week, but they also worked hard and I can't recall anyone ever drinking in the office, let alone being drunk or unable to do their job. And, however much time was spent in the pub, we always looked smart. I wore a suit and tie every day I worked at Harrap. Sports jackets (quite often tweed, and with leather elbow patches) were admissible if there were no external meetings, and most of the women wore long skirts.

FAMILY OWNERSHIP AND MANAGEMENT

Paull Harrap was the Managing Director and Chairman of the business. It had been founded by his grandfather George in 1901, and management had simply passed down the male line of the family. When I was there, Paull Harrap would have been in his mid-50s – affable and well-educated, a gentleman publisher. He certainly enjoyed the idea of running a publishing company, even if he didn't actually do much. As far as I could tell his principal duty was to chair a fortnightly weekly of senior managers in which publicity spend and book prices were agreed. Other than that, he seemed to have little involvement in the day-to-day running of the business and rarely fraternised with the staff, preferring the company of authors and associates at his club. There were several other Harrap family members and in-laws who would occasionally be in the office and were associated with the business, though their roles were often unclear. The company and its assets were entirely owned by the Harrap family, without any external shareholders.

I was perfectly happy at Harrap, but chose to leave largely for financial reasons. The economy was struggling and in 1973 the government had introduced a mandatory pay and prices freeze in order to tackle high inflation. This meant that it was very difficult to get a salary increase without changing employer. I had a young and growing family and needed to earn more. The only options were to get a big promotion with a new job title, or else change companies and try to get appointed at a higher rate of pay. And so, with some sadness, I scoured the pages of *The Bookseller* and tripped over an editorial job at Pergamon Press in Oxford.

Not many years after I left Harrap & Co, the company was sold to Nick Berry, youngest son of Lord Hartwell and member of the dynasty that had owned the *Daily Telegraph* for much of the last century. Although the Harrap name remained, this ended any of the family's ownership or financial involvement with the firm. Whatever plans he may have had, it wasn't long before Nick Berry split the business and sold the education titles, reference and dictionaries to the Scottish publisher Chambers, while the trade books went elsewhere, eventually disappearing into part of Virgin Publishing, under the control of Branson's brother-in-law, Robert Devereux. In the 1980s, Chambers-Harrap was acquired by Havas, the French advertising and communications group. Havas in turn became a subsidiary of the global media corporation Vivendi, which sold its entire European book publishing operation, including Chambers-Harrap, onto Lagardere, a diverse multi-industry conglomerate, headquartered in Paris but with operations in territories around the world and which today has upwards of 30,000 staff. Lagardere had interests ranging from retail to automobile engineering before undertaking a corporate restructure in the 1990s to focus on media and entertainment. As part of this, it sold many of its existing businesses and acquired a number of publishing and media titles, many of which were brought together. This included the prestigious Parisian publishing company Hachette, which is where the very last books (a range of English-French dictionaries) bearing any vestige of the Harrap name still reside. It is a not atypical saga of the demise of a family-owned independent publisher.

FAST FORWARD FIFTY YEARS: LAST DAY AT THE BLOOMSBURY OFFICE

Nearly fifty years later, in May 2018, I left the office of Bloomsbury Publishing in Bedford Square, after my last day as a full-time employee. I walked home as I might have done nearly fifty years earlier. Unlike my last day at Harrap, I barely had any belongings to carry out – almost everything of importance was stored electronically.

This office was no more than half a mile from Harrap's old building, but in every crucial respect it was completely different. It has been observed by sociologists that in the first three decades after the war technology radically altered the home, but that in the three decades after that, it transformed the office. This was as true of publishing as any other industry.

The Bloomsbury office was composed of three inter-linked buildings in Bedford Square, with four floors, a basement and a conservatory used for parties and meetings. There was a PC on every desk, and also phones – but these were hardly used, people preferring email and their own mobiles. It's also worth reflecting on what wasn't there in either the Harrap or Bloomsbury office. Half a century is a long time when the pace of change is so fast, and there are a range of devices that had never been imagined back in 1972, but which had been invented, widely used and then rendered obsolete within my fifty years – there was no microfilm reader, laser disc player, Dictaphone, telex or fax machine to be seen.

Unusually for a modern company, the Bloomsbury offices were not open plan – in this respect, it was more like Harrap than many other publishers in 2018. Commissioning editors and directors had their own rooms, but many of the other staff also shared offices. There were approximately two hundred staff based in the office, of whom probably more than 70% were women. Of the senior executives and departmental heads, roughly two thirds were women – including such key roles as editor in chief, head of rights, marketing, international sales, legal, production, and finance. Many of the staff were themselves shareholders – it was a publicly-listed company, and staff were given incentives to own shares. Although some individuals may have been members of a union, there was no recognised trade union and unions in general played no part in corporate thinking. Apart from a few sales reps who were expected to be out on the road nobody had a company-funded car.

There was obviously no warehouse on the premises and no booksellers would ever have thought to turn up at the offices to order their books. The stock was predominantly held in a warehouse in Swansea. There were still lots of printed books around – the front reception desk room was lined with shelves of Bloomsbury's books, but this was for presentational reasons rather than having any commercial function.

Few people bothered with ties, even for external meetings. Women largely wore trousers or shorts in the summer, and trainers or ballet flats. Many of the staff would turn up in their cycling gear, shower and change into more comfortable work wear for the day. If they were going out in the evening straight from the office, for instance to a book launch, they might then change again into something more glamorous. Drinking at lunchtime was very much the exception rather than the rule and the Bloomsbury offices certainly didn't reek of cigarette smoke – by this time, even smoking outside within the vicinity of the building was discouraged.

Harrap's office had been much the same in 1972 as it would have

done at the dawn of the twentieth century, but was different from Bloomsbury's in ways that would have astonished the likes of Paull Harrap or
Roy Minton. In the course of fifty years a publisher's offices, as well as its
staff, working culture, business practices and much else besides, have been
transformed. I would witness much of this, and in my own way even help
to make some of it happen, though the route would be a circuitous one.

CHAPTER TWO: THE BRAVE NEW WORLD OF SCIENTIFIC PUBLISHING

Headington Hill and the domain of Chairman Maxwell; a crash course in scientific publishing; life sciences and a brief vision of the future; an abrupt and unhappy departure; the not-so brave new world of Oxford University Press; fine dining at Ely House; tea ladies with trolleys; decision-making at the world's largest university press

At the beginning of 1974 I arrived at the gates of Headington Hill Hall, located in the east of Oxford, in my new job as Publishing Manager of Biological Science at Pergamon Press. Robert Maxwell had sold the business he founded to Leasco some years earlier but then, in uncertain circumstances, had raised the finance to buy it back and was now in full control again. My first day coincided almost exactly with this and, having had nothing to do with my appointment, I well remember him striding towards me that morning, demanding to know who I was and what I was doing in his office. As a 24-year-old editor, this was an intimidating moment. Maxwell was already a well-known figure by this time, having been a Labour MP, and had started to cultivate the persona that would be such a feature of public life for the next twenty years. He was well over six feet tall and, even in those days, a man of substantial volume and presence. Before I could fully explain what I thought my role was, he told me, not unkindly, that I clearly didn't know the first thing about publishing, but that was okay because he would teach me everything I needed to know.

When I joined, Pergamon had about 300 staff, more than three times bigger than Harrap and substantially more profitable. It immediately felt very different – this was a proper hard-nosed commercial organisation. My starting salary was £3000 and it rose to £3800 over the course of the year, but it was a time of high inflation and such sizable increases didn't count for much. Biology included agriculture, life sciences and, sometimes, medicine. Peggy Ducker, senior editor and editorial heart of the business, helped run things, but Maxwell's presence was everywhere. It was important to him that he was always referred to as the Chairman, but he was far from being a non-executive Chair.

In the years that he'd been away, Maxwell felt that Pergamon had become overly bureaucratic and lethargic, and he wanted to bring back the dynamism of an owner-manager to the business. This began every morning at 8.30, when the editors and management would assemble in the post room and the mail was opened by Maxwell himself. It was an important ritual, intended to encourage the kind of entrepreneurial mind set he wanted to instil in us. He would open an invitation to a biochemistry conference in Vienna, and demand to know who was going to secure the rights to publish the proceedings. Or he would hold up a leaflet advertising flower seeds and insist that we get them to advertise in one of our botany journals. We needed to find a commercial angle to every piece of correspondence, and speed of response was critical.

There was an in-house journal, the *Pergamon Gazette*, which would

Volume 1 Number 1 of the Pergamon Gazette

carry the Chairman's column on its front page. As Maxwell made clear in the augural edition, "To be frank, on my return to Pergamon Press, one of the first facts that struck me was the virtual breakdown that had taken place in internal communications." He was good to his word but with Maxwell, communications tended to only go in one direction: not long after I started, a loudspeaker system was installed throughout the building, so that we could receive all-staff messages over the course of the day. "Attention. This is your Chairman speaking..." would be a frequent interruption to our working lives and, whatever we were doing, we were expected to stop and listen. Even if we had wanted to, it was impossible to ignore the booming voice. Decades later, when Oxford Brookes University was refurbishing the offices, a mass of wires above the ceiling were found, and it is quite possible that the Chairman was not only broadcasting, but also listening in on us.

Maxwell's overbearing personality was also reflected in Pergamon's physical offices, which were organised around his home, Headington Hill Hall, and which is now home to Oxford Brookes University's School of Law and Centre for Publishing. The Hall itself was spectacular, built on the slopes of Headington Hill in the early 19th century Italianate style, and since the 1960s, Maxwell had leased it from Oxford City Council – he liked to call it "the best council house in the country". It was here that he lived, worked and entertained, and staff (especially young secretaries) would constantly come and go between his home and the Pergamon buildings. His office in the Hall was suitably magnificent, with steps at the back leading down to a terraced lawn and swimming pool. On an enormous table all of his various affairs would be arranged in different piles: business matters, but also his political affairs, financial interests, social correspondence. He would work his way through them more like a cabinet minister than a company executive. There was also a much smaller table on which there would be a chess board, with the pieces permanently set out in mid-game. I later found out that they had been deliberately arranged in the form of a particularly fiendish opening, in order to impress visiting European scientists and politicians, many of whom were expert chess players.

Within the grounds of Headington Hill, the main Pergamon offices were modern by the standards of the day and well designed. This was an open plan layout, with more than a hundred people working on the same floor. There were also stables that had been converted into offices, which is where I started. There was a bar and table football, so, as young editors, we would socialize and drink there. Coming here from Harrap was like jumping forward decades at a time. It felt like switching from a low league football club to a top professional outfit, with all the facilities, equipment and support services one needed to do the job well. There were no pigeon holes and we could make telephone calls, even international ones, anytime we wanted.

Maxwell had a perfectly good management team, but their jobs were almost impossible. Gilbert Richardson and Eric Buckley were joint Managing Directors, with Alan Stevens the Finance Director, who would become miserably embroiled in Maxwell's labyrinthine financial affairs. Richardson and Buckley had been running Pergamon in Maxwell's absence during the Leasco years, but when Maxwell returned, he quickly reasserted his authority over them. They were both kind and able men who tried to serve Maxwell loyally, only to discover two decades later that their pensions had been appropriated and squandered.

One of the most instinctive entrepreneurs I have ever met, Robert Maxwell could hardly have been more different from Paull Harrap. He would bring an invoice to the accounts department and instruct them to convert all invoices from British pounds into Swiss francs because he thought it would come in at a more favourable rate (he was in essence betting against sterling, which at the time was not a bad idea). Always alert to business opportunities, and with an enormous personal network, he managed to secure Pergamon the lucrative contract to produce the training manuals for North Sea Oil rigs.

He increased by five-fold the price that Pergamon charged for the re-use of its illustrations, while at the same time getting rid of the entire department responsible for managing and enforcing this. Instead, he issued editors with a rubber stamp, which just said something along the lines of "You have permission to use, on payment of $50." The editors would simply stamp the letters of request and they would be returned to the sender, without even making a copy. His intuition (again, correct) was that most people would just pay the higher rate, and that it wasn't worth the cost of pursuing those that didn't. He had a hatred of overstocks and would reissue hardbacks as paperback editions, with stickers saying 'paperback' brazenly affixed to their obviously hardback covers. In all aspect of the business, he had no compunction about making tough, even brutal, decisions and was relentless in seeking out inefficiencies and chasing up new deals.

15

PUBLISHING AND THE LIFE SCIENCES

As part of his continuous horizon scanning, Maxwell took a particular interest in his Biological Science Editor. At an all-company meeting, he held up the famous Nature paper by Crick and Watson on the structure of DNA and announced that it had changed our business. Requesting that I stand up, he declared that this young man was going to lead our publishing in life sciences and that, more portentously, the future of academic publishing would be in this area rather than the physical sciences, which up until then had been Pergamon's main strength. Maxwell had grasped that developments in the field had come to a point where there was going to be an explosion of research, and therefore publications, across the life sciences – particularly in molecular biology, genetics and biochemistry. At the same time research in disciplines such as astronomy and sub-atomic physics would fail to keep pace, owing to the enormous costs now required for experimental research. He was, of course, quite right and in the next year alone Pergamon launched almost a hundred new textbooks and journals in the life sciences, which were technically my responsibility. The titles initiated by Pergamon would become the heart of the business and its chief revenue generator. It was why Maxwell was later able to sell his company to Elsevier for several hundred million pounds, and many of these journals are still at the core of Elsevier's profitability today.

A good example of Maxwell's instincts (albeit not in the life sciences) is the journal Tetrahedron, which is still published weekly and read across the world. It has been the principal journal of organic chemistry research for more than sixty years and has played a crucial role in shaping its field. Its history of contributors is littered with illustrious scientists and Nobel laureates, but few now remember that its origins lie in Robert Maxwell writing a speculative letter to the professor of organic chemistry at King's College. He had spotted the famous 'gap in the market' and, unlike some gaps, it needed to be filled.

LEAVING PERGAMON IN ABRUPT CIRCUMSTANCES

Chairman Maxwell was known for his swashbuckling management style and he revelled in this reputation – often liking to sack people abruptly and publicly. On one occasion, in front of many of the staff, he brutally fired the international sales manager for having returned from a sales trip to India with an order for only fifty sets of a pharmacology encyclopaedia. Given each of sets was selling at $1000, this hadn't seemed to the rest of us a particularly bad result. As Pergamon grew and he became richer and more powerful, the shouting and workplace bullying got worse. When he moved across into newspapers, it was no surprise that his mistreatment of editors soon become notorious even by the standards of Fleet Street.

One of his other great flaws was an inability to make any kind of distinction between his business and personal life. It was only when his empire collapsed twenty years later that the full scale of this would become apparent, along with its disastrous consequences for so many who had worked for him. But the warning signs were there back in the 1970s and it would also be the cause of Maxwell and my falling out. Curiously, though, it arose not from a professional matter or because of any editorial decision, but rather in my role as Father of the Chapel of the NUJ. It was the second General Election of 1974 and Maxwell was standing as a Labour MP, trying to regain the parliamentary seat of Buckingham that he had lost in 1970. Rather dubiously, coaches had been booked to take the entire Pergamon workforce out to the constituency in order to canvass on his behalf. He might have been the Labour Party candidate and so in principle supported by the union, but to impose such a three-line whip on his staff was unacceptable, and it was my unenviable job to have to tell him so. Maxwell's response to being challenged in this way was predictable: "You could have a good future here, but not if you behave like this."

When I refused to give way on the issue, my fate was sealed – but at least it was done with some discretion and there was no public humiliation. Rather, a week or so after our encounter, Maxwell's fixer, a shadowy figure called Aubrey Chow, came to find me in the coffee room with a copy of The Bookseller, showed me an advert for a job at Oxford University Press and advised me that I should think about applying. I took this, as it was meant, to be a message to leave as soon as I could. My career at Pergamon, intense and instructive as it had been, had lasted less than a year.

For all the difficulties of working for Maxwell, I was dismayed to be going. Pergamon had been a stimulating place to work, and there had been some talented editors and publishers there to learn from. The office on Headington Hill was a beacon of innovation at a time when science, and scientific journals in particular, were still something of a backwater in British publishing. More than almost anyone else, it was Maxwell who transformed this into a cutting-edge industry of international importance. He was able to do this partly because he understood scientists and academics better than any publisher before him. Although he had no training in the biological sciences, he closely followed developments in the field and, more importantly, knew the value of networking, of being charming and flattering researchers. A committed internationalist fluent in several languages and with connections across Europe, Maxwell cultivated relationships with eminent scientists, university administrators, funders and librarians around the world. To be taken out for lunch at expensive restaurants and treated to drinks in London clubs was an enjoyable novelty for many of these people.

It is no surprise then that, whatever his staff may have thought of him, Maxwell was a great favourite in much of the scientific community, many of whom had supported him in the days when he had been wrestling with Leasco for control of Pergamon. It was common for the academic editors of Pergamon's most prestigious journals to be appointed directly by Maxwell himself. This was the case with the biggest journals that I worked on, such as Comparative Biochemistry and Physiology and Progress in Neurobiology, both of which were edited by his friend, the zoologist Gerald Kerkut. As part of the arrangement, Maxwell contributed towards the costs of what, for an academic, was an unusually lavish lifestyle, including in Kerkut's case the setting up of a charitable trust for the university of Southampton. Maxwell had no compunction about doing these kinds of deals, and he reaped the rewards with the launch of new journal titles, valuable commissions, subscriptions, book contracts, favourable licensing agreements and much else.

And, notwithstanding everything that happened afterwards, Robert Maxwell was a brilliant publisher. His personal flaws might have already been on show by the mid-1970s, but so were his talents. At

Pergamon in 1974 there had been a real sense of change, of technologies opening up and new ways of disseminating scientific research, and this was largely down to him. It also should be said that it is for these same reasons that for many in the Open Access movement, which was to emerge as a force twenty years later, Maxwell is regarded as the founding father of the kind of scientific publishing that they so wanted to reform. But for good or ill, he changed publishing and it would be some years before I experienced anything quite like it again.

THE NOT SO BRAVE NEW WORLD OF OXFORD UNIVERSITY PRESS

Within a few weeks of my conversation with Aubrey Chow, Maxwell had failed to get elected as the Member of Parliament for Buckingham, and I had been hired as an editor at Oxford University Press. I had been offered the role of Biological Sciences Editor after a brief interview with the publisher, Dan Davin, at Balliol College. But this was subject to approval by OUP's Biology Delegate – Rodney Porter, Professor of Biochemistry and future Nobel Laurate. Professor Porter interrogated me about the future of molecular biology. Fortunately, at Pergamon we had recently published a book on catecholamines and, although I had only the faintest idea what they were, I used the term frequently enough for him to be satisfied.

But shortly before I actually joined the job was changed to that of Medical Editor – an offer I immediately accepted, as it was at the larger salary of £4000. This was because the person they had actually wanted, a certain Tim Hailstone, had at the last minute turned them down on the grounds that it wasn't enough money – although, as I discovered a few months later when I met him for the first time, it transpired that he had turned down £7500. Much of my career has subsequently been spent admiring Tim's ability always to earn twice as much as me.

Within OUP, medical publishing had long been seen as a professional rather than scholarly endeavour, and so was based in London along with children's books and general publishing. For a while I commuted from Oxfordshire to Ely House in Mayfair. This was inconvenient with a young family, but the arrangements at Ely House had their compensations. OUP leased the entire building, with a fine library overlooking Dover Street, expertly looked after at one time by Deborah Moggach who went on become an acclaimed novelist. There were three dining rooms – one in the basement for all staff, which provided hearty and generously subsidised fare, while on the second floor there was an officers' dining room, reserved for editors and middle managers, where meals were prepared by a fine chef and the drinks were free. At the very top of the building was the publisher's dining room, which was exclusively for the use of the head of the London office, Sir John (Bruno) Brown, and his guests. The food here was sourced from Jacksons of Piccadilly and the wine list was excellent, with the cellar being overseen by a senior manager at OUP whose job involved spending at least a month in France every year researching and ordering directly from *vignerons*.

As Publisher at OUP, Sir John (Bruno) Brown was already something of an industry legend. He had been an overseas sales manager for OUP before the war and, after the fall of Singapore, captured by the Japanese where he got to know a British Council officer, A.S. Hornby. To pass the time in prison camp, ASH, as he was known, had been devising an English dictionary that could be used by non-native English speakers. Brown saw the commercial opportunity and took over the project. Published in 1948 and sold ever since, the Oxford Advanced Learners Dictionary of English is not only the world's best-selling dictionary but has a credible claim to be the most profitable book of the 20th century.

Yet even this wasn't enough to save the London office. In the first of many painful cost cutting measures, the office in Mayfair was closed and medical publishing and everything else moved to Oxford into the famous building on Walton Street. While this was not as salubrious as Ely House, it was (and remains to this day) an immense and impressive building, with its neoclassical façade and quad giving it the appearance and character of an Oxford college. We didn't have three different dining rooms, but there was still a subsidised canteen at the Clarendon Press Centre – a staff club nearby with a snooker table, cheap drinks and a colour television where we could watch cricket during extended lunch breaks.

Compared to Pergamon, the OUP headquarters felt like a step backwards in time. There were about ten senior academic editors, all arranged by subject – medicine, history, philosophy etc – and all, with the exception of Vivian Bone, were male. We sat in small individual offices along the same floor in what was known as 'death row'. There were probably no more than five science editors (including maths and medicine). This reflected OUP, and indeed Oxford University's, historic strengths in the humanities as opposed to the sciences, something that would partly change over the following decades. The secretaries, all female, shared their own room. There were also tea ladies with trolleys, who would come through the office in the morning and afternoon to serve us hot drinks, buns and biscuits. Class distinctions permeated throughout the organisation, in every possible form and detail. There were even two sets of bike racks in the quad – one for the 'scholars' or editors, while the other was for those who worked in printing.

Editors were defined by their subject area, and it was their job to understand the sector and to have in-depth knowledge of who the leading academics were, how the field was evolving, and which researchers potentially had a good book in them. The subject area distinctions had to be observed – it wouldn't do for a maths editor to interact too much with philosophers and vice-versa. Unlike at Harrap or Pergamon, editors would have little to do with production and much would of course depend on how dynamic an editor was. It was very easy to sit back. Generally regarded as the most prestigious university press in the world, there was always a danger of complacency and the assumption that the most promising authors would come to us rather than the other way round. It was typical of the culture of OUP that, when my predecessor Clifford Gregory retired as medical editor, he rather dispiritingly told me: "I don't envy your task, because all the best books on medicine have already been published."

Once a manuscript had been submitted, it would be reviewed and approved or otherwise by the OUP Delegates. If the editor wasn't happy with it, he would send it back to the author with a note to try again, with minimal editorial guidance. If it was acceptable, a 'pink slip' would be issued to the printer: "To the printer, from the publisher RDPC: please print 2000 copies", and that was more or less the last you saw of it until the copies arrived at the warehouse (although that was to change radically). There was a quaint, and in many ways admirable, rule that authors were forbidden from thanking their editors by name in the acknowledgements of their book. This was on the principle that everyone in the company, from printer to editor to post room clerk, had contributed to its production and so no individual should be singled out for praise. Not a bad rule when I read some of the Oscar-winning lists of thank yous in many books today.

DECISION MAKING AT OXFORD UNIVERSITY PRESS: A BEGINNER'S GUIDE

Oxford University Press was and is a wholly-owned asset of the University of Oxford, and it discharges its duties through the Finance Committee, which is the closest thing it has to a company board. The chief executive of OUP would sit on this committee along with senior staff, half a dozen academics at the university and one or two business figures. The Finance Committee in turn reported to the Delegates – in fact, the chief executive still goes by the dual title of CEO and Secretary to the Delegates. In my time, there were approximately fifteen of these Delegates, responsible for the reputation of the Press and quality of the published works. Editorial decisions were made by the Delegates at fortnightly meetings along with senior OUP staff and one or two relevant editors in attendance, all under the chairmanship of the Vice-Chancellor of the University.

When I worked there, these meetings would take place at 11am every other Tuesday, apart from just one during the (very long) summer vacation, which unfortunately meant that few editorial decisions or contracts could be issued for three months of the year. The editors would gather at the OUP office, don gowns, walk to the Clarendon Building on Broad Street, and were expected to be there ahead of the Vice-Chancellor who would arrive flanked by proctors. We would all stand on his arrival and everyone, editors and Delegates, wore robes. The meeting would then proceed around an enormous table, with inkwells replenished with fresh ink and reference books, including *Who's Who* and *Crockford's Clerical Directory* to inform discussions. With perhaps one or two exceptions, every meeting I remember was attended entirely by white men.

The Delegates were all academics, each representing a different subject and matched onto an editor – so every editor had a Delegate partner, whom they needed to work closely with. The Vice-Chancellor would go through the list of book proposals and provided the editor had done their job properly, their partner Delegate was already fully on board with the book, and would make sure it got passed, supporting the editor and defending it if necessary from fellow Delegates. A traffic light system was introduced while I was there to make it clear if the editor thought the proposed book would be unprofitable but reputable and hence worth publishing, break

22

even or even be profitable. Each proposal would be discussed at length and books would be 'ploughed' if deemed not publishable. There was an apparatus for voting but I can't recall it ever being used, with the Vice-Chancellor seeking to achieve a consensus and the Delegates generally happy for someone else's books to get approved provided their own did. But there could still be lengthy debates, and difficulties would arise when a proposal didn't have a Delegate associated with it, in which case everyone then felt entitled to have their say. A biography of Beethoven generated the greatest controversy that I can remember. There was no Music Delegate, but the Economics Delegate at the time took a keen interest in Beethoven and strongly championed the book. However, the Medicine Delegate also regarded himself as well informed in classical music and felt that enough biographies of Beethoven had recently been published. A long and increasingly ill-tempered discussion took place, at the end of which it was eventually decided, much to the Economics Delegate's dismay, to plough the book.

By half past twelve, it was usually the case that the Delegates would be getting hungry and we would have discussed no more than twenty books, with anything up to another fifty to go. For this reason, one of the editors' tricks was to try to make sure that the books that they really wanted to publish were always towards the end of the list – for instance, by playing with the alphabetical order of authors in multi-author books. With lunchtime calling and attention wandering, it was almost guaranteed that the last dozen or so books would be swiftly and unanimously passed through, along with the education, reference, English Language Teaching and children's books, which always came last and were barely discussed despite the fact that, in financial terms, these were the most significant decisions to be made. And after that, with the meeting finished, the Delegates would disperse to their colleges and the editors would stagger off to the pub. I'd like to think that this tradition, at least, is still maintained.

Decision making at OUP might have been tortuous but that didn't mean that an editor couldn't make things happen. In fact, something not always appreciated is that, compared with trade and fiction, there is often scope to be more pro-active in academic publishing – to spot a market opportunity and commission an author or even a new series to meet it. Just such a moment came when I had been over-seeing the publication of *Price's Textbook of the Practice of Medicine*, a standard reference work that stretched back more than half a century, but which had lost much of its lustre. The twelfth edition had come out in 1978 and promptly been hammered by a well-known American reviewer who ended his critique with the memorable sentences: "I couldn't help but notice that the distinguished editor of this work is physician to her Majesty the Queen. God save the Queen."

Duly chastened, and despite the warnings of my predecessor that all the best medical books had already been published, I took it upon myself to visit the Nuffield Professor of Medicine, David Weatherall at the John Radcliffe Hospital. I brought the damning review with me and suggested that he should take on the task of producing a completely new textbook. Sir David (as he later became) conscripted two co-editors to undertake this mammoth task with him, and they in turn commissioned individual authors for different subjects. Four years in the making, the *Oxford Textbook of Medicine*. came out in 1983 - a large-format, 2000-page, multi-volume work that sold for £55 (today it is priced at over £400). Used by medical students and physicians worldwide, it has since sold hundreds of thousands of copies, with its sixth edition released in 2020, and generated much-deserved royalties for the editors for the last 40 years.

CHAPTER THREE:
A TIME OF CRISIS

*Economic crisis and no bail out, cost-cutting and out-sourcing; a plan
for innovation and renewal; Dictronics and first encounters with
computers; the decline of Oxford's paper and print industries; the
Oxford English Dictionary Second Edition; another abrupt departure.*

It was the early eighties, and the British economy was in a state of crisis
and upheaval. Long-standing firms, institutions that had been major
employers and the bedrock of towns across the country for a century or
more were facing existential challenges. Many of them would no longer
be there by the end of the decade. This was as much the case with publishing as any other industry, and it was particularly the case with Oxford
University Press.

Much of what OUP was experiencing was similar to the problems at
the British Leyland plant, across the city in Cowley. There were enormous
and long-standing inefficiencies that were getting exposed as the economy internationalised. No longer able simply to circulate their products
around the remnants of the old Empire, British publishers were facing
up to competition from North America and particularly Europe, where
businesses such as Springer, Kluwer and Elsevier were leading the field in
academic publishing. Much of British management was suffering a profound malaise: dominated by a generation of men who greatly respected
traditional hierarchies and had little in the way of business and financial
skills. At OUP, as elsewhere, many of them had served in the war, and
wartime experiences were still a staple topic of conversation at staff drinks
and dinners. These men were often distinguished classicists and humanities scholars, but struggled to adapt and innovate. Difficult decisions were
constantly postponed while powerful unions, especially in the print in-

25

The Executive Committee of OUP in 1978 (l to r Don Webster, Jimmy Huws Davies, Raymond Brammah, Byron Hollinshead, David Mitchell, Sir John Brown, Vivien Ridler, George Richardson, Dan Davin, Eric Buckley)

dustry, were thwarting reform and the adoption of new technologies. The media were frequently running stories about the British brain drain, and how creative, scientific and business talent was seeking better opportunities across the Atlantic. Inflation in 1981 was running at over 10% and unemployment touched three million, while at the same time, North Sea oil revenues meant that the pound was unnaturally strong on currency exchanges making UK exports less competitive.

OUP was the largest university press in the world, it had recently celebrated the five hundredth anniversary of printing in Oxford and it was in danger of going bankrupt. There was an overdraft limit of £12m with Barclays and the company was close to breaching the covenant. The Secretary to the Delegates had been told by the bank that in order to have the overdraft extended, there would need to be a 'letter of comfort' from the Vice Chancellor of Oxford University. But upon receiving this request, Sir Rex Richards let it be known that he would 'not sell the slightest bauble in the Ashmolean to save OUP'. It would be entirely up to us to sort ourselves out.

This was the context in which I was asked, much to my surprise, by the executive team to write a paper to suggest some ideas for getting us out of our predicament. Nowadays, this would have been done by McKinsey for several hundred thousand pounds but instead I was given six weeks to consult with senior managers and editors across the organisation, and the only budget was for the sandwiches I bought from Oxford's Covered Market for lunch with colleagues (around £5 in total). The seven-page typed document that resulted from this probably lacked sophistication and had little in the way of infographics, but it didn't pull many punches.

The fat had to be cut, particularly in terms of buildings and people. There had to be much more accountability within the organisation and localised profit centres. Distribution was far too expensive and incredibly slow, while the printing had become antiquated, inefficient and unaffordable. And we had to focus on the markets of the future rather than the past – which meant moving away from Bibles and self-serving trade book publishing and more towards reference, journals and English language teaching. Perhaps most significantly, the paper was intended to challenge the entire culture of the organisation. At the senior levels of OUP there was an assumption (and, I thought, a profound misunderstanding) that general book publishing should be profitable, while academic publishing was done for scholarly principles, and couldn't be expected to make money. In fact, as Oxford-based competitors such as Pergamon and Blackwell were demonstrating, this wasn't the case. The company was being run on the basis of cross-subsidisation, a lack of financial accountability and a belief that certain things could carry on losing money for as long as other titles and departments continued to pay for them. It was this, more than anything else, which had to change.

My first strategy document, 1984

27

COST-CUTTING, UPHEAVALS AND OUTSOURCING

One of the first things to go was the warehouse complex in Neasden, which was shut down and relocated to Corby in Northamptonshire where a smaller but much better designed facility was built, employing 200 people. A peculiarity of Corby is its distinctive Scottish population and character – a legacy from the 1930s when the Glasgow-based Stewarts & Lloyds constructed one of the UK's largest steel works there. As Scottish steel declined in the 1960s, Scottish steel workers moved south to find work. But by the early 1980s, steel making in Corby had come to an end as well, causing significant unemployment. The government was offering generous grants for businesses of any kind to relocate there and OUP, with its own financial problems, was happy to take advantage.

The printing division was broken up in stages. Typesetting was largely outsourced to cottage industries such as Hope Services, based in Clifton Hampden just outside Oxford. Hope had the capacity to use the latest range of IBM typewriters that produced 'camera ready copy' which could then be photographed and used as a printing plate. By today's standards, this is a rather primitive technology, but it was a step change from the letterpress that had been used by the OUP works. One complication was that the print workers refused to print anything unless it had been certified by the Society of Graphical and Allied Trades (SOGAT), which by this time had become the country's dominant print union. This meant that we still needed to pay for all of the plates to be stamped by a SOGAT affiliated company before they could actually be printed. But even with this additional hurdle, it was still far cheaper than the previous arrangement.

So, after five hundred years, printing at OUP came to an end. Thankfully, some of those working in the printing divisions were able to move across into publishing. Up until the 1980s, roles that we would now consider to be core publishing industry jobs – production, jacket design and copy editing – were sometimes undertaken by printing companies. This was very much the case at OUP, which meant that, for much of the nineteenth and twentieth centuries, it was at the print works where you would find many of the country's finest copy editors. This included characters such as Leofranc Holford-Strevens, a legendary Oxford figure who could speak more than forty languages and, so the story goes, translated a passage of ancient Greek into Serbo-Croat during his Classics finals, as the exam paper had failed to specify it should be translated into English. Although regarded as one of the outstanding classics students of his generation, his eccentric personal habits precluded him from academic life, even at Oxford in the 1960s. Nevertheless, he found a long and happy home at OUP – firstly within the print works and then, after the reorganisation in the 1980s, within publishing itself. A leading American academic in medieval music was so impressed with the editing of her monograph that she travelled from New York to meet and then promptly marry him. By the time Holford-Strevens retired, he had worked on more than 500 books, correcting the typographical, and factual, errors of the world's most renowned historians and classicists.

But not every job could be saved in the same way. Since the 1940s, OUP had had a cartographic department, with up to twenty mapmakers and apprentices who produced geographic atlases and maps for textbooks. The department was well known for the technical quality of its work, with its maps to be found in school rooms across the world. It had also pioneered the production of 3-D maps and techniques for representing the relief of territories. But map making was an expensive and highly specialist activity, and in 1981 the department was closed and OUP did what nearly every other publisher had done and subcontracted to dedicated cartographic firms. Happily, many of the staff went on to establish Oxford Cartographers, a firm that is still running today.

Bible printing and publishing was struggling too. There was a dedicated warehouse in Jordan Hill on the edge of Oxford for Bibles and prayer books and which also received all of the damaged and soiled stock that had been returned from OUP's booksellers around the world. Given that the Bible was the 'word of God', the strict rule at Jordan Hill, which was staffed largely by Christians, was that none of these returns could ever be pulped. Inevitably, over the decades, many thousands of unsellable Bibles had accumulated there. The problem was eventually resolved by selling off the site to a developer who used some of the land and money to build a smart new sports pavilion and, as part of the deal, took possession of the damaged stock – which ended up, it is thought, buried beneath the M40 motorway that was then under construction.

It wasn't just a case of shutting things down and outsourcing – there was a huge (and long overdue) pressure on margins throughout the business. We had to pay close attention to the costs and overheads of what we were doing. For instance, at the time we used to print a quarter of a million copies of the *Concise Oxford English Dictionary* every year. By changing the formatting and presentation of the phonetic alphabet on to the end papers, we were able to remove 16 pages of copy, the equivalent of an average editor's salary (not to mention, several tonnes of CO_2).

For all the pain of restructuring and cost reductions, it was also a time of renewal and innovation. Amidst the redundancies and the cost cutting, there were also new opportunities arising. My boss and mentor Dan Davin retired as Academic Publisher and was replaced by Robin Denniston who, despite being a part-time Anglican minister, showed sharper commercial instincts. In his previous role at Hodder and Stoughton he had published John le Carré and many other bestsellers. He knew how to make money from publishing and he well understood the need for OUP to rescue itself and become financially stable.

Robin encouraged and promoted talent and new thinking. Amongst the editors and managers, we established the 22 or 'second eleven' com- mittee – a generation of publishers mainly born after the war who were excited by what was happening in the industry, and wanted to bring the innovations seen elsewhere to OUP. Nor was it just men. In 1982, we appointed the 25-year-old Kim Scott Walwyn as commissioning editor for English literature. Kim, who died tragically before her time, was one of the most brilliant editors I ever worked with, and it is testament to both her talents and the new managerial culture that Robin was fostering that within a few years she had become editorial director for all of the humanities. It was Kim who tracked the numbers and tried to understand what was driving sales. It was becoming possible through OUP's systems to request reports on different territories and subject areas and while most editors would be fixated with getting their books reviewed in the *TLS*, Kim (whilst as keen on the TLS as anyone) unpicked the data to see if this actually helped sales or not (it usually didn't) and would try to focus resources on what worked. The term 'data analytics' didn't exist then, but for Kim and the new generation this was very much part of the future. We would meet in The Gardeners Arms pub to talk about this and also new markets, production technologies, marketing techniques and other developments that were changing the face of publishing. One of the most important of these, although it wasn't mentioned at all in my strategy paper, was computing.

FIRST ENCOUNTERS WITH COMPUTERS

The first computer I was aware of, without actually ever seeing it, was at the offices of Harrap which arrived some time in 1973. It was in the finance department and everyone in editorial suspected that it was being used to monitor our expenses. Whatever it did or didn't do, the machine never impacted upon us directly and it never came up in the course of work. Sales figures were calculated by going to the production department to ascertain how many had been printed, going to the warehouse downstairs to check how many were left in stock, and then checking with publicity as to how many had been given away. With some analysis and a lot of guess work, you would try to come up with a figure of how many copies had been sold. It was such a laborious and approximate process that you would only do this when you were meeting authors and knew that they were going to ask. But you still had a sense of how well the book was doing: if the warehouse was running out of stock and you had a reprint request, then it was selling well. If not, not.

The words digital and technology are now used almost synonymously, but for the first decade of my career, there were a range of technical innovations that had little or nothing to do with computing. In my brief time at Pergamon, I came across several of them, for Robert Maxwell was a great enthusiast for new inventions and took pride in ensuring that his business was equipped with the very latest devices and gadgets. I didn't see many computers in my time there, but we did make extensive use of one of the quintessential publishing technologies of the 1970s – the microfilm.

To anyone much under the age of 50, the microfilm will mean almost nothing, in much the same way that the fax machine is a mystery to anyone in their 20s. But it was one of the most talked about technologies of its time. As people started to worry about the information explosion, so microfilm was seen by libraries, institutions and even consumers as a solution to housing the ever-more published material. Improvements in film, and the advent of smaller, portable scanners and readers all seemed to herald an era in which the traditional book form, bulky and expensive to produce, distribute and hold, would be no more. The entire works of Shakespeare could now be photographed and kept on a single film that could be stored in a small box and viewed with a handheld device. The text wasn't searchable and all you could do was read it, but it was still seen as a revelation, in the same way that the CD-ROM would generate similar levels of excitement twenty years later.

At Pergamon, microfilm was not just an end product, but rather used as part of the production process. An enormous form (a primordial version of the Biblio publishing management system of today) would be typed into on special double-size typewriters to create a single huge sheet. This contained all of the information, what we would now call meta data, which the publisher needed in order to produce a book: author, title, ISBN, royalties, print run, contract etc. This form was then photographed, shrinking all the information onto a microform, which could then be accessed by a microform reader at the various production stages. Whether it actually made things any easier I'm not sure, but it certainly felt modern and radically more advanced than anything I had encountered at Harrap.

Another technological innovation which I saw for the first time at Pergamon was the 'word processor'. As everyone knows, for the last forty years this has been a software program that runs on general purpose computers, but back then a word processor was actually a specialist machine, best thought of as a sort of hybrid between typewriter, printer and computer, albeit with limited functionality. Robert Maxwell acquired several of these at great expense not long after I started at Pergamon, and was incredibly proud of them. On one occasion, never forgotten by all those who witnessed it, he was gleefully showing them to East Europe officials who had come to visit the office. Eager to demonstrate that these enormous contraptions could be folded up and easily stored, he attempted to do exactly this by folding up the entire table that one of the machines was bolted onto. A man of considerable size and strength, he actually succeeded in this: lifting and folding, and naturally breaking, the table and machine.

These innovations were all hints of a world to come, but it would be at least another five years before digital technologies would start to change things. At OUP in the 1970s, as in so many other ways, modern technology had yet to make an impact. As with Harrap, all of my correspondence was typed by a female secretary whom I would dictate to, and the fact that secretaries were equipped with IBM Golfball typewriters was seen as a notable advance over the traditional typewriter. There were no photocopiers, these wouldn't appear until the 1980s, and so the secretaries would make three carbon copies – one to be sent out to the correspondent, a copy for the editor's file and then what were called 'thirds' – a common filing system that all staff could access at any time, like a sort of paper-based intranet. Unlikely as it seems, people would regularly go through this, and it was probably used more than any number of corporate intranets and knowledge sharing systems that I would encounter in later decades.

So it wasn't until the 1980s that I had my first real encounter with computer technology, and it came about for a very good reason – we were desperate to make money. It was the winter of 1981, OUP was struggling financially and I was expected to help do something about this. It was at this time that I came across an article in *Publishers Weekly* describing how a company improbably called Dictronics had struck a deal with Random House to make the first computerised dictionary. Intrigued, I rang Dictronics and got through to their founder, Dick Brass, and told him that if it was dictionaries he was interested in, then he really needed to be speaking with OUP.

Dick was interested enough to invite me to New York and then, after I admitted that I had no travel budget given our financial stringencies, agreed to cover the cost of my ticket provided I travelled between Christmas and New Year, when the flights were cheaper. And so, at the very beginning of 1982, I found myself on the 8th floor of a ramshackle Manhattan building. Dick had been the restaurant critic at *Playboy* magazine, when his experiences with early computers had made him wonder how they could make writing easier and more efficient. He had founded Dictronics as a software firm that tracked accounts and generated threatening letters to debtors, but now he was looking to do more ambitious things. Apart from Dick himself, the team consisted of a son of a Conservative government minister, a single programmer who wrote all the software and Andrew Rosenheim, a talented copywriter and editor.

They showed me the first floppy disk I had ever seen. The thing that most struck and puzzled me was that the box was far too big for the disc, in which it rattled around. It transpired that this was because Dick Brass's father supplied the packaging from his textiles factory two floors above in the same building, and that they had actually been intended for women's stockings. Nonetheless, there was a deal to be done and we agreed that Dictronics would pay us $600k (with $200k up front) for the rights to computerize and sell three reference books, including the Pocket Oxford English Dictionary, all of which would be re-keyed and put on floppy discs. It was the first deal of this kind I had ever done. The means of distribution would be what became known as bundling – people buying a computer would receive the reference works on disc as part of the package. In the 1990s, millions of people would get Microsoft's CD-ROM encyclopedia *Encarta* in the same way.

All of this was highly innovative and ahead of its time – the computer market in the US, both for home and business use, was still in its infancy. The idea was that people using early, primitive word processors on their computers could consult their floppy disc version of our dictionary. For Dictronics, it was a huge risk and investment, but one which paid off – not long afterwards, Dick sold his business to Wang Laboratories, at the time one of the world's biggest computer companies, who used what he had created to launch the first electronic spellcheckers. Dick went onto become Vice-President of Microsoft and is regarded as one of the founding fathers of electronic publishing in the US. Back in Oxford, eyebrows were raised in certain quarters about what we were getting into, and concerns were only heightened when Dick came to visit and, treated to dinner at St John's College, refused the fine wines on offer from the cellar and insisted on drinking Diet Coke. But given the state of OUP's finances, no one could argue and Robin Denniston was thrilled. Having signed the contract, Andrew Rosenheim moved over to the UK on behalf of Wang to oversee editorial production, and then came across to OUP and has been in Oxford, and a good friend, ever since.

THE TRANSFORMATION OF PRINTING

The first book printed in Oxford was in 1478, two years after William Caxton introduced the printing press to England. On this basis, OUP claims to be the oldest university press in the world – although naturally, this is a source of controversy and there is a competing claim from Cambridge University Press. Whatever the exact date, for most of its history, OUP was more a printer than a publisher of books, and this was still very much the case when I joined in 1975. Probably 80% of the building was dedicated to typesetting, printing and binding. At the beginning of my time there were probably around 700 staff in total, and my estimate is that 500 of these worked in printing. But the title of 'printer' is something of a misnomer and they would do a great deal more than simply print books. They oversaw the copyediting, typesetting and proof reading and the editors themselves would have minimal involvement in the actual production.

In contrast to OUP, Harrap's printing had been largely done by small independent printers – principally J.W. Arrowsmith in Bristol, who would undertake the typesetting, printing and binding. A Victorian printing business, Arrowsmith produced diverse offerings including labels for Harvey's Bristol Cream sherry and lives on, in name at least, through the *Arrowsmith's Bristol Channel Tide Table*, which has been published continuously since the 1830s. Books for Harrap would be delivered to the building in High Holborn and stored in what was the warehouse on the ground floor. Of course, to the reader now, the idea of using a prime central London location for the storage of books would doubtless seem extraordinary.

Perhaps even more surprising from the vantage point of 2022 is the fact that, until the mid-70s, OUP didn't just print books, it also made its own paper. In Wolvercote, upstream on the river Thames on the northern edge of Oxford, was the company's paper mill. This was where, since the seventeenth century, the paper had been produced to supply the print works. In particular, the mill produced the thin, tough paper, known as India paper, used for Bibles and prayer books. In a forerunner of the up-heavals that would be coming, the mill was sold in 1977, and not long afterwards three hundred years of paper making in Oxford came to an end. For a while, the old mill house was inhabited by a succession of for-tunate OUP employees on a peppercorn rent, but the entire site is now a private housing development, with three-bedroom houses there selling for upwards of a million pounds.

Looking back, the end of OUP's in-house printing seems inevitable. Not only were these sizable print works located in one of most expensive cities in Europe, the printing had become more and more uncompetitive. The printing division remained almost entirely reliant on a steady pipeline of work from OUP: general and academic books and journals, bibles and prayer books. Apart from papers for examination boards, it had few exter-nal clients. With all this work guaranteed, there had been little incentive for the print works to innovate, adopt new technologies or cut waste.

It wasn't until the 1970s, that OUP had abandoned hot-metal type-setting. Elsewhere, commercial printers were competing for publishers and contracts and being forced to become more efficient, while at the same time new competitors emerged from across the world as countries industrialised – the more forward-thinking publishers of the time, such as Paul Hamlyn, were already making links with printers in Czechoslovakia and China.

But the end of printing at OUP was a cause of much sadness. The city of Oxford's character has always been shaped not just by its world-famous university but also its industrial heritage and skilled manual labour. For hundreds of years, OUP's print works had been an essential part of this. In the course of the nineteenth century, the Jericho neighbourhood had grown to become a vibrant working-class area of terraced brick houses and corner pubs, built for the printers who lived and socialised round the corner from work. Generation after generation had worked there, from apprenticeship through to retirement. As happened to so many manufacturing workers in Britain at the time, many of the printers who lost their jobs struggled to find work elsewhere, their specialist technical skills of little value in the 1980s labour market. Nowadays Jericho itself has become a highly desirable location, much favoured by professionals for its central Oxford location and proximity to the train station. Other than in the names of local pubs such as The Old Bookbinders and The Rickety Press, almost all traces of its printing history have disappeared.

One of the consequences of the changes in printing, is that print runs from previous decades now come across as strikingly large. One of my earliest books at Harrap, *The History of Quantum Theory*, translated from German, highly technical with masses of equations had a print run of over 2000 – not much different from the first print run of a novel and about ten times more than would be the case of a similar tome today. This was by no means unusual. At OUP we would do monographs of a standard 2000 copies – although whether the copies were ever despatched let alone bought or read is a matter for conjecture.

Print runs were so large for reasons of cost. Typesetting a single page cost £10 in the money of the day, and corrections were £1 each. By today's standards, this equates to £120 and £12. *The History of Quantum Theory* with its 260 pages would cost approximately (in 2022 money) £35,000 to typeset alone. Reprints were similarly expensive and the temptation was always to have a large initial run rather than a number of smaller ones. The book sold for £6.10 or just over £73 in today's money – perhaps roughly the same as an academic monograph would sell for now. Given the huge outlay, it is easy to understand why editors were incentivised to go for large print runs, with results that can still be seen in warehouses and second-hand book shops around the world.

THE OXFORD ENGLISH DICTIONARY SECOND EDITION

On the basis of the Dictronics deal, and the fact that no one else knew the slightest thing about computers, I was now regarded as OUP's digital production expert. In fact, so poor was the general knowledge of digital technology throughout the industry at this time, I had even become Chair of the Publishers Association's first Electronic Publishing Committee. It wasn't so much that people weren't interested (although there were plenty in publishing who weren't) but that no one was remotely knowledgeable. A publisher with a background in computer science or information technology was rarer even than a natural scientist.

And so I was brought into one of the great publishing projects of the era – the second edition of the Oxford English Dictionary. The OED, published in volumes between 1884 and 1928, is regarded as one of the monumental achievements of British scholarship. Originally conceived by the Philological Society of London in 1857, it was envisaged to be a four-volume work that would take ten years to complete. In fact, after five years they had only reached as far as the word 'ant' and it would eventually require many hundreds of editorial staff working over half a century, with the voluntary assistance of thousands of amateur scholars – famously one of its most prolific contributors turned out to be serving a life sentence for murder in Broadmoor asylum. The first edition of the OED is therefore rightly regarded as the stuff of legend and its story has been celebrated in books and films. But the second edition, produced very differently, would also be a milestone in publishing history – and computing technology would be central to it.

If the Dictronics deal had been done for the money, the OED was initiated for the values of scholarship and the glory of the English language. But also for the money. By the early 1980s, the OED was coming to the end of its copyright period and so if we didn't hurry up and make a new edition, the rights would become available to every other publisher. This was the time of the 'dictionary wars' with Harper Collins, Longmans and Penguin all eyeing up the reference book market and thinking that

Oxford's long-held supremacy in dictionaries was there to be challenged. Since the final volume of the OED had been released in 1928, there had been a small number of updates in the form of large supplementary volumes, but it was now agreed that a complete new edition would have to be produced.

A project of this magnitude required considerable resources. A supervisory board was established that included professors of English, Philip Larkin, the Vice-Chancellor Rex Richards and Umberto Eco, among others. The then chief editor of the OED was Robert Burchfield, who had been tutored by C.S. Lewis and J.R.R Tolkien and had been working on supplements to the OED since 1957. He was a distinguished lexicographer and scholar, but with little interest in modern publishing – he was sceptical of new technologies and was opposed to introducing digital production methods. Nor was he alone – across OUP and the university more generally, people tended to be anxious about computers, and had the feeling that digital information was intangible and at risk of being lost. In fact, the far greater risk was that the physical records that were the basis for the dictionaries would be damaged. A building in the city centre, with minimal fireproofing, held all of the paper slips that had been used to compile the various editions of the OED – handwritten notes providing definitions and citations for words, supplied by thousands of individuals over decades, none of them copied or backed-up in any other form.

Despite the resistance across Oxford, it was clear that any new edition would require computing expertise and, given the prestige of the project, we were able to put together an impressive consortium to address this. A sales representative from IBM called Bob Corwin was trying to get OUP to install a new telephone network with them, but when I asked him instead if he could help us with the OED, he immediately saw the publicity opportunity and brought in John Fairclough, Director of IBM UK and later the government's chief scientific advisor, who agreed to give us £2m worth of equipment and expertise. When Fred Dainton, chair of the British Library, heard about this, he was sufficiently excited to have a conversation with Prime Minister Margaret Thatcher, and not long afterwards we received a grant of £350,000 from the Department of Trade and Industry towards the project. Meanwhile, over a dinner in Oxfordshire I met the Vice-Chancellor of the University of Waterloo, Canada's leading centre for software and linguistics, and who agreed for his university to become the software partners. Finally, Reed Technology and Information agreed to do the typesetting from their facility in Philadelphia, mobilising 120 typists to key in almost 60 million words (twice to enable a merge and purge operation), all of which were checked by more than 50 proof readers in Oxford.

All of this was a far cry from how the first edition of the OED had been published, or indeed how OUP had ever done things. An international consortium, which combined the traditional editorial excellence in Oxford with a range of partners who could provide the latest computer hardware, production skills, finance and software. It was an immense undertaking but, unlike the first edition, it came out on schedule and upon its launch in 1989 was immediately regarded as one of the great publishing events of the time. There were 290,000 entries over 20 volumes, using more than two million quotations from English language sources – 33,000 from Shakespeare alone. It remains the authoritative guide to how the language has evolved over the last thousand years to the benefit of scholars throughout the world. There were at least four CD-ROM versions and then in 2000 it was made available online. It is now updated four times every year, with several hundred new words added each time.

TRYING TO LEAVE OXFORD UNIVERSITY PRESS

By the mid-1980s, OUP was no longer losing money. The costs and inefficiencies, particularly those associated with printing and production, were being tackled. Meanwhile, dictionaries and reference were expanding, and the lucrative ELT market was growing stronger by the year and would continue to do so, especially as Eastern Europe started to open up. The management culture was also changing – with its generous pension packages, senior managers tended to leave as soon as they turned 65, creating space for younger publishers to move up the ranks. But much about the institution of OUP would continue to frustrate and hinder progress, and ultimately I left in unhappy (for me at least) circumstances.

In 1987, the chief executive George Richardson was approaching retirement. A search committee was established and chaired by Sir Roger Elliott, the Wykeham Professor of Theoretical Physics. By now, I was Managing Director of the Academic and General Division and applied for the top job, as did the finance director, Bill Andrewes. Both of us were interviewed by the search committee, which was made up entirely of OUP Delegates such as the distinguished historian Sir Keith Thomas – but no one with any business experience. I was not yet 40 at the time and I thought there might have been a concern that if I was given the job at a relatively youthful age, I would be in place until my retirement, more than 25 years away. When I told Sir Roger that I would only do the job for a maximum of ten years, this failed to satisfy the committee – although I was later told that this was because he had misheard me, and thought that I had been asking not for a 'ten-year contract', but rather for 'tenure'.

Eventually, after an interminable and confusing process, Sir Roger announced that his committee had failed to find anyone suitable, and so had decided that he should take the job instead. After twelve years it was time to go. I spoke to Paul Hamlyn on the phone and, although he was no longer directly running his business, Octopus, he said that he would find me a job. That was good enough for me, and I left that very day.

Or rather I tried to – as with so much at OUP, leaving wasn't straightforward. Neither Robin Denniston nor George Richardson (my boss and my boss's boss) were available (it was a Friday afternoon after all), and the Personnel Director refused to accept my resignation on the grounds that he was not senior enough to accept it. The only possibility was to find the ultimate boss. And so, by now in a state of desperation, late in the afternoon, I dashed over to Wellington Square and to the Vice-Chancellor's office. I was relieved to find the VC, Sir Patrick Neil, still there and he was surprised to see me. I explained my desire to resign and he kindly expressed concern that I was leaving when I didn't have another job confirmed. When I told him that Paul Hamlyn had offered me something, his response was sniffy to say the least – "Have you got the offer in writing? Paul Hamlyn, isn't he just a street trader?" I told Sir Patrick that I trusted a street trader rather more than the University of Oxford, and made my goodbye.

There was one more thing to do. I returned to the OUP office and wrote my formal letter to the Vice-Chancellor. In this I declared that I was putting my name forward for the forthcoming vacancy of Chair of Theoretical Physics at the University of Oxford. I acknowledged that "While it is true that I have not studied physics since 'A' levels, I do have a general interest in the subject. I realize that the University would be inclined to appoint someone from within the ranks of established physicists but I would like my candidature to be taken seriously." After all, I continued "If you were to appoint one of the excellent physicists available this would be seen as slighting to the others. Therefore, it would be appropriate to appoint someone with very little knowledge so that they are all equally slighted." Furthermore, I pointed out that as someone who wasn't close to the subject, it would be "a real advantage to have someone with a fresh perspective."

It was only many years later that Viv Smith, my secretary at the time who had typed the letter, revealed to me that she had never actually sent it to Sir Patrick. In her wisdom, she had judged that it might not be of benefit to my future career.

CHAPTER FOUR: THINGS SPEED UP

The house that Hamlyn built; paperback publishing; 1980s management speak, company cars and corporate decadence; the Millwall Football Club of British publishing; academic vs trade and the importance of making books about camels; going back to school; the hazards of dealing with literary superstars; the quite different hazards (and much bigger rewards) of celebrity publishing.

I had first met Paul Hamlyn in the early 1980s. As usual, OUP was in financial trouble and Robin Denniston, who knew Hamlyn well, had taken me to meet the great entrepreneurial publisher at his offices in Octopus Publishing Group in Grosvenor Street. The hope was that we might come up with some projects that might quickly make money for the Press.

Hamlyn was an insatiable and inventive deal maker and exactly the man we needed to see. We sat down with him and his colleague, Jonathan Goodman, to talk through some ideas. In little more than an hour, we had come up with two agreements that were 'good to go'. Octopus would license OUP's World Classics series, to produce attractive, smaller hard copy versions of our titles at an affordable price. They were also interested in our reference and natural history titles, such as the *Oxford Book of Birds* – although in this case, he wanted to produce larger-format versions which made the most of their illustrations. These were nice deals – getting the OUP brand out to bigger markets and distribution channels. Octopus would pay an advance, but what should the royalty be for OUP? Negotiations had happened so quickly that neither Robin nor I had considered this, and so I plucked a number out of the air and said 25%. Hamlyn fell off his chair, rolled with laughter and said he'd give us 5%, and we shook hands on 10%. All in all, it had been a very productive afternoon.

Hamlyn and I stayed in contact after this. He lived in London during the week, but liked to spend the weekends at his country house in Gloucestershire. His driver, Colin, would drive him up in his Bentley on Friday afternoons and, as a man in his 60s, he needed a convenience break along the way. He got into the habit of stopping off at the OUP offices most Fridays, halfway en route for a pee, a machine coffee, and to talk publishing. In this way, I got to know him well and he became something of a mentor to me.

There is little doubt Hamlyn is one of the greats of twentieth century publishing. Born in Berlin in 1926, he came to Britain as child when his family escaped the Nazis, and began his career after the war, selling books out of a wheelbarrow in Camden. He was as enterprising as Robert Maxwell, but without the monstrous egotism and disastrous personal flaws. Although publishing in a different field, like Maxwell he had the same talent for spotting market trends and emerging business opportunities. In the 1960s, he had anticipated the growing affluence and more sophisticated tastes of Britain's burgeoning middle classes and so helped to invent the concept of the 'coffee table book' – handsomely produced large-format titles on art, design, interiors, food and other lifestyle subjects. His books made extensive use of colour illustrations and photographs at a time when such printing was still expensive and he distributed them not just in bookshops, but in supermarkets and the new home accessory stores that were starting to appear on the high street. He had the same consumer insight, admiration for good design and attention to production values as his great friend Terence Conran, and in the 1980s they jointly founded Conran Octopus, publishing attractive books on interior design, gardening and cookery. A tough negotiator, but widely admired for his honesty and gentlemanly conduct, he championed liberal causes and made major donations to the Labour Party and the Bodleian Library. Unlike Maxwell, who spent his wealth on yachts and football clubs, he established the Paul Hamlyn Foundation, which more than twenty years after his death continues to support arts, culture and young people.

When I met Hamlyn, he was well on his way to making his second fortune. Having spent twenty years growing his first company, Paul Hamlyn Books, he sold it to IPC (part of Reed International) and then in the 1970s started out all over again with Octopus. He made a series of brilliant commercial deals – WH Smith wholesale were his distributors, and he negotiated the price and the quantity on highly favourable terms, while at the same time he had managed to secure low-cost, high-quality production from Czechoslovakian printers. But by the 1980s Hamlyn was impatient to grow the business further and faster and after raising investment from Owen Green at the BTR conglomerate, he used the funds to go on an ambitious spending spree. In a short space of time, he bought Heinemann which included Secker & Warburg and its share of Pan Books, Heinemann Education and Ginn. He bought Websters, a small chain of bookshops which in turn owned the Bookwise Extra wholesaler. He also bought Mitchel Beazley, the reference and lifestyle publisher with a range of best-selling titles including Hugh Johnson's wine books series and *The Joy of Sex*. He even bought back his original company, Paul Hamlyn Books, in 1986. Fascinated by the commercial opportunities in Asia, he somehow found the time to set up a print brokerage in Hong Kong, which he called Mandarin Offset after the hotel he liked to stay in.

Growing this quickly was risky and created a fair amount of chaos, but it paid off, and in 1987 he was able to sell the entire Octopus group to Reed International for more than £500 million. Reed was a long-established printing and packaging company, a classic British business originally founded by the Methodist family it took its name from in the 19th century. It had grown steadily over the decades into something of a conglomerate, owning among other things Crown Paints and some wallpaper businesses. But during the late 20th century the company transitioned into publishing, acquiring the IPC magazine group in the 1970s, jettisoning its printing and selling off its paint and packaging operations. With its corporate strategists anxious to cement itself further as a major player in international media, it had bought out Octopus and all of its publishing and bookselling interests at a price which many in the industry (including me!) considered excessive.

The great benefit of all this was that it enabled the establishment of the Paul Hamlyn Foundation, an endowment today worth in the region of £800 million and which gives out tens of millions of pounds each year to arts and education causes. And on a more personal level, it meant that when I started at Reed International shortly after their purchase, there was plenty of work to do.

THE WORLD OF TRADE PUBLISHING

Given the speed with which Hamlyn had grown Octopus before selling onto Reed, there were myriad businesses, brands, imprints, partnerships, licences and agreements that needed bringing into order – in many cases, it seemed that no one fully understood what had been bought or agreed to, and it was far more chaotic than I had expected. Although it was a relentlessly commercial, publicly-listed business and in theory therefore had an onus on efficiencies and margins, it was actually far less organized than OUP, which had always been a highly structured institution. Reed International Books had some ten different royalty systems that needed to be turned into one. This was far from straightforward – building a royalty system is one of the most sensitive things that you can do in a publishing company, and a sure-fire way of alienating your biggest assets, the authors. The mantra repeated by executives in every meeting at the time was 'synergy'. This was very much 1980s management speak, but with so many different businesses and brands – covering book publishing and distribution to travel information, magazines and consumer events – everyone was certain there must be scope for cross-sector collaboration and making efficiencies. Yet finding genuine synergies was easier said than done.

Paul Hamlyn himself was no longer managing things, although he was still involved as a Reed board member. My boss was the pugnacious Ian Irvine, an experienced media executive now in charge of Reed International Books. Ian was a blunt northerner, the scourge of inattentive waiters and unprofitable editors, and by no means universally popular. He was not a book publishing man (which didn't endear him to editors), and had originally come from the accountancy firm Touche, which has since merged to become Deloitte. But he had been the perfect foil to Hamlyn, with his close scrutiny of the finances complementing Hamlyn's intuitive gift for deal making, and he brought rigour to all parts of the business – "that's the square root of bugger all" was a phrase you would often hear from him, and he was invariably right.

In my first management event at Reed, which was held to my amazement in the splendour of the Gleneagles hotel, there was a talk by a colleague I knew from my OUP days, Bill Mitchell. He was now running the children's division and, having come from a very different part of Reed, he said that he could make disinterested decisions. At this Ian was heard

The board of Pan 1986 (l to r Ian Irvine, Simon Master, Nicky Byam Shaw, ? can check, Paul Hamlyn, Nicolas Thompson)

to mutter: "So the fucker isn't even interested in the business." Within a week, Bill was gone, for it seemed that Ian didn't recognise the difference between uninterested and disinterested. It's fair to say that this was not something that would have happened at OUP. Yet for all his belligerence, he could always be trusted to keep his word and, provided you had the nerve to speak your mind, he would listen and respect your opinion.

The first job Ian gave me was to establish a new paperback imprint. The back story to this was suitably tortuous. Heinemann had had a 50% stake in Pan paperbacks, along with Macmillan. When Hamlyn sold Octopus, this triggered a clause hitherto unnoticed by anyone at Reed, allowing the other party (i.e. Macmillan) to buy out Reed's stake at a price set by an independent arbiter. Nicky Byam Shaw, the CEO of Macmillan, was one of the few to have actually read the contract and offered £20m, which was less than Reed wanted, but satisfied the arbiter. The upshot to all this was that Reed had now lost its paperback imprint, and it was my job to set up a new one, and to grow it fast enough that it was capable of competing with Pan and other paperback houses. It was called Mandarin, and alongside it we had Minerva for literary titles and Mammoth for children's books. Given that we had a pipeline of new titles from Heinemann, Secker and Methuen, as well as everything else across the Reed group, there were soon plenty of rights coming our way. We were also taking on titles that had previously been licensed to others, but whose paperback rights had elapsed and so could now revert to us.

The first paperback we published was an early export edition of a title from Heinemann. Early exports are paperback editions that are sold in certain outlets, mainly airport bookshops, prior to going out on general release, in order to get to the European market before overseas (principally US) editions. I knew to price it in line with the US edition, but had no idea at all what the print run should be. I hadn't long been out of academic publishing, and had never heard of the author or title. In the end, after a drink with a sales rep, we plumped for 10,000 copies. The book in question was *The Silence of the Lambs* by Thomas Harris and all of the copies duly sold, as did a further million or two after the release of the movie.

Reed International was a FTSE 100 company employing over 15,000 people including about a thousand in books. It was a proper global business with offices in Australia, North America and Singapore. The qualms at OUP about travel budgets certainly didn't apply here, and staff moved frequently between offices and countries. Nor was there the same resistance to modernisation or anxiety about technology: computers had yet to hit editorial departments, which were still based around typewriters, secretaries and vast amounts of paper, but they were starting to transform back-office systems. There were plenty of problems with all this. For instance, we learnt that one of the reasons that the (mainly male) wholesale book reps at BookwiseExtra had worked so well was because they had travelled around the country in vans full of stock, flirting with the (mainly female) bookshop staff – a modernised, teleordering distribution system was not what any of them wanted, and our sales initially collapsed in the parts of the country where we introduced it.

While there was still little ethnic diversity in the UK, Reed was a far more feminine place than anywhere I had worked before. For the first time there was a generation of women who weren't purely in administrative roles. The trade books side of Heinemann was run by Helen Fraser, Children's by Ingrid Selberg, and across the group there were women in senior positions – in editorial, but also in sales, marketing, rights, finance and production. There was undoubtedly still a glass ceiling, and until the 1990s there wasn't a single major publishing company with a female chief executive, but things were definitely moving in the right direction.

Our main office was the stunning Michelin House in Chelsea, built in the Art Deco style at the turn of the twentieth century. This was owned by Paul Hamlyn and Terence Conran, and it was very much to their taste. The building was arranged around an atrium, and everything was light, clean and uncluttered – to the point that we were even discouraged from having too many books in the office. There was a very good restaurant,

Bibendum, along with a Conran shop, oyster bar, wine bar and a highly profitable florist – Hamlyn had clocked that we were close to a number of private hospitals. The wine bar was where we met our authors – it was here that I first got to know Bill Bryson, and it was a particular favourite of the likes of Oz Clark and Hugh Johnson. Nor was it just wine – from time to time, colleagues and authors would come out of the bathrooms at Bibendum, noticeably more lively and talkative than when they had gone in.

The days of colleagues playing snooker, drinking beer and watching cricket were gone. Work and socializing were much more blended and book launches became social events in their own right, with publishers expected to set aside proper budgets for them. At the same time, with the arrival of Waterstone's on Britain's high streets, bookshops were becoming more like social venues, capable of hosting events and readings. But not everything had changed, and I was still happily smoking in the office.

BAD BEHAVIOUR IN THE ROARING 80S

It was the late 1980s – after the stagnation of the 1970s and economic crises of the early 1980s, these were the boom years – at least if you were lucky enough to be in one of London's fast-growing white-collar industries. It was an era of lower income taxes, deregulation, corporate expenses, long lunches and business class flights to international conferences. The fact that Reed was a public listed company, and so ultimately answerable to shareholders for our expenditure, certainly didn't hold anyone back. My welcome dinner at Reed to meet the other directors and their wives was held at Le Manoir aux Quat'Saisons, then (and now) one of the most expensive restaurants in England. The next year the senior team went to the Four Seasons in Florida for management workshops, and we were all given gold cufflinks, marked 'R' for Reed from the luxury jeweller Asprey. I was delighted because the R could also stand for Richard and I still wear them to this day. Another year, we all flew out to visit the famous MIT Media Lab in Boston, to hear a talk by the futurologist Nicholas Negroponte, who was then one of the most high-priced public speakers in world. He told us that the future of print media would be three dimensional, as it had more surface space and so could transmit far more information.

Meanwhile over at IPC magazines editorial expenses had become a major part of the running costs. One executive had the bright idea to shame the most profligate editors by ranking every magazine in a monthly table of total expenses and circulating it throughout the company. Unfortunately, and perhaps unsurprisingly, expenses rose even further as the editors of the likes of *Marie Claire*, *New Musical Express* and *Country Life* vied to be the number one.

These levels of corporate lavishness now seem faintly extraordinary, and it certainly wasn't anything I had experienced before – nor indeed, very much since. But, much as when I worked at Harrap, from the perspective of 2022, probably the thing that jars the most is the car culture. Ian Irvine drove a Bentley, and everyone remotely senior had an expensive car, paid for by Reed. Cars have never been my thing, and it all seemed a bit pointless as our offices were in central London and I rarely had to travel the country, but I was still given first a Jaguar and then a bulky BMW model, which at the time was the preferred vehicle of home counties' drug dealers.

Even more striking than the cars themselves is the fact that every executive director at Reed International would have their own driver. At the corporate headquarters in Chesterfield Gardens there was a chauffeurs' room, where a dozen or so of them would hang around all day (and night), waiting to be called. At OUP, there had been a single in-house driver who would take directors, and anyone else that needed a lift, to the airport, but at Reed even I had my own personal driver, Martin – and if Martin was unavailable then his father would sometimes drive me. By now we were living in Chelsea and, having little use for car or driver, I would often lend them out to authors – a certain former Australian PM, whose memoirs we'd published, would make use of Martin when in the country so that he could be taken down to Wales to see an old female friend. Paul Hamlyn enjoyed travelling in luxury as much as anyone. He had a Bentley and a succession of drivers, all of whom were expected to take the name Colin, so that he didn't have to trouble himself remembering a new name. When it came to the Frankfurt Book Fair, Colin would set off two days ahead in the car so that so that he could then pick Hamlyn up from Frankfurt airport and drive him around.

Undoubtedly, far worse was happening in industries such as advertising and finance, but somehow this new kind of corporate culture and excess seemed more unpalatable in publishing – a profession that in the popular imagination was still populated by well-educated, genteel men in corduroy jackets. *Private Eye* would regularly run stories about how this new breed of publisher was bullying editors, and even the editor of *The Bookseller* magazine rather unkindly chose to print the most unflattering photograph he could find of Paul Hamlyn and me, drinks in our hands and looking like a pair of plutocrats.

Such attacks on Reed International in particular were common for, in many ways, Reed was the bad boy of late 1980s British publishing. My colleague, Sandy Grant once said to me in a rather improbable analogy: "Reed is like Millwall football club. They all hate us and we don't care." And it's true that in some ways this was the company culture – we were instrumental in helping to dismantle the Net Book Agreement; we (temporarily) left the Publishers Association; and we were relentless about reverting paperback rights. Paul Hamlyn had been hugely respected and liked in the industry but, although he was still around, he was no longer managing things. Instead, we had Ian Irvine, who attended one Society of Bookmen dinner and managed to quarrel with so many people that he refused to attend again, nor was he invited. But Reed was also unpopular in the industry for structural reasons. The company had grown with a strong commercial impetus – Paul Hamlyn hadn't so much set out to be a publisher, but rather to make money from publishing. He had started out, after all, not making books but selling them on the streets of post-war Camden. All parts of the publishing supply chain were of interest to Reed – from printing in China through to running the London Book Fair, and we were vertically integrated in a way that was unusual at the time. This meant, for instance, that we owned a 50% share in BCA (Book Club Associates), which at its peak had four million members and was one of the biggest buyers of books not only from Reed, but most British publishers. In certain markets, Reed was therefore both a competitor to other publishers as well as being a customer or supplier of services, and this was a situation that was bound to arouse suspicions.

The demise of Bookwise Extra was an unfortunate example of this. Owned by Reed, for a time it was the UK's biggest wholesaler of books, but attempts to impose a more centralized structure on the business had backfired, and it went bust owing almost every publisher in the country a great deal of money. Reed at least was able to take back its stock at a penny a copy, which would reduce royalty obligations, but other publishers were not so fortunate, and the episode did little to endear Reed to the rest of the industry.

ACADEMIC VS TRADE PUBLISHING

After fourteen years largely in academic and educational publishing, it took a while to accustom myself to the different sensibilities of 'commercial' publishing and, in some ways, it is something that I struggle with even now. Within my first year at Reed there was a management conference (there were many of these) and this included a light-hearted quiz in which we had to nominate the worst book that we had published that year. I was shocked and, in my naivety, found myself feeling slightly outraged by this – at OUP, an editor would have thought it unfathomable that they had published something 'bad', a book whose merits they weren't prepared to defend. We would happily joke about the obscurity of a book's subject matter or its dismal sales figures, but never would we admit to it being of a poor quality, or produced to shoddy editorial standards.

It was while at OUP that I had overseen the publication of probably the lowest selling book I was ever involved with, *The Anatomy of the Dromedary*. Launched in 1987 to a largely oblivious world, I think it barely reached three figures in sales. In truth it was probably never going to be one of the great sellers, but to compound matters, it was a book about the totemic animal of North Africa and the Middle East written by two Israelis and a South African. But crucially, it was the only anatomical guide to the one-humped camel (they are very difficult animals to dissect) and up until then there had never been a detailed study – nor, I think, has there been one since. In other words, the scientific community needed this book. It transpired that this was actually a very small community, but there had

Screenshot from Amazon

still been a feeling that this need should be met. No one at OUP faced any kind of reprimand for publishing such an obvious commercial dud – it wasn't how editors were generally judged. It should also be added that, in early 2023, a second-hand copy of the book is on sale on Amazon for $1500 – even more than the totemic Madonna's *Sex*.

OUP had been extravagant in its own way, at least in my early years there – and Ely House had been especially spectacular. But rich dinners and fine wines at college dinners tended to be the height of our excess, and I certainly can't remember anyone disappearing into the toilets and coming back agitated and unable to eat their food. Running up expenses, first-class international travel, luxurious company cars – these were all frowned upon. It wasn't simply a case of more restrictive rules or a different ownership structure. Rather, for all its flaws, OUP has always had an institutional culture: the rule that editors could not be personally thanked in an author's acknowledgements seems odd, but it also reflected the sense that many people had work to produce a successful book and so no individual should be singled out for credit. And perhaps this helps explains why, despite all the frustrations of OUP at the time, so many brilliant editors and publishers continued to work there. It also goes some way to explaining why, however bad things may have got in the early 1980s, the company was able to get itself out of its hole, and ultimately become a major contributor to Oxford University's financial as well as intellectual health.

In my experience the very best publishers are motivated not so much by money but because they love the business of publishing – people want to be paid well, but there are other important considerations and rewards, and a good publishing company will provide these. But the overriding imperative at Reed was to make money, and this was to become ever more the case over the years I was there. There was a strict corporate target to increase profits by 15% every year, and we were all incentivized to meet it, even though this risked corroding our asset base. This meant that we sometimes sold perfectly good publishing businesses that we should have built up further, in order to hit this relentless target. It is no wonder that problems arose. For instance, Reed's Travel Group, had always been a successful, standalone part of the business – publishing travel guides, timetables and hotel directories. But in the late 1997, there was a scandal, when it was discovered that executives had been exaggerating circulation figures for the previous five years – advertisers had to be recompensed and Reed Elsevier's share price was badly hit. This is exactly the kind of thing that happens if the corporate culture is exclusively a financial one: people become anxious of their positions, overly competitive with colleagues, prone to covering up their mistakes – or even worse, start to make things up.

Another important difference is that at Reed, there was no formal recognition of a trade union, and unions in general played no role in our decision making – whatever the question, at no point can I recall anyone ever saying "what will the unions think about this?" I had been father of the chapel for the NUJ at both Harrap and Pergamon, and while I had switched to the management side at OUP, unions were always considered. It was a reflection of how the UK had changed over the last period but was also because by this time Reed, despite having started as a Victorian newspaper printer, no longer had any in-house print works. Printing was done in the UK at various independent printing concerns and, after the Iron Curtain came down, increasingly in Eastern Europe. Furthermore, Paul Hamlyn had from an early stage seen the potential for doing business in China and by the early 1990s we were already printing in China, operating out of our office in Hong Kong. As the decade progressed, more British publishers would do the same.

In stark contrast to OUP, Reed was a place where management, and managerial skills, were taken seriously. There was investment in professional development, clearer structures and incentives, and far greater accountability. There were performance-related bonuses and, as a publicly-listed company, many of the senior managers had shares. Undoubtedly the strong competitive ethos could be damaging, and it meant that editors and managers frequently moved jobs, but it also meant that performance and accountability were clearer, and that managerial progress could be made much faster than at OUP.

By 1992 I had become head of consumer operations, in charge of all of trade books. Ian Irvine was chairman of Reed, which meant that I was in line to take on all of Reed International Books. However, it was agreed that I needed more management training before I could take it on (something that was inconceivable at OUP), so in the autumn they paid for me to go on the Harvard Business School's Advanced Management Program, an executive training course. And so, twenty years since starting work I was back living on a university campus, as a student again at the age of 42.

Of the 120 or so of us on the course, I was the only publishing executive apart from a chap who ran Yellow Pages in New Zealand. Half of the students were US executives, and on the whole less entrepreneurial and more risk averse than the Europeans, and were much more likely to have a legal background. Probably the single most important thing I learnt was that if there is a part of your job that you really dislike then you shouldn't do it. This was a revelation to me. Up until then, I had always had the Puritan notion that you were paid to do things that you didn't enjoy doing. But the business gurus at Harvard told us to focus instead on doing the things we enjoyed, because we were most likely to be good at them, and ask other people to do the things we didn't, as they were bound to be better at it.

It's been an enduring lesson for me. To take an example, the part of management I had always found most tedious was office planning. Many thousands, if not millions, of pages have been written about how offices can be best arranged to improve staff productivity, internal communication, job satisfaction and much else. But it is never something that ever bothered me, and I have been equally happy in modern, open plan, purpose-built offices or rickety converted townhouses. When it comes to company politics, few things are more deadly than arguments about the position and size of a director's office – although back in the 80s, of course, it was parking spaces that everyone rowed about. But ever since my time at Harvard, I've always found a colleague who is interested in, and even enjoys, overseeing office arrangements (you'll be surprised how many there are) and have left them to do it far more effectively than I ever could.

THE PERILS OF LITERARY PUBLISHING

Although I had been in publishing for twenty years when I started at Reed, literary editors were a new experience for me, and one that took some getting used to. They had an attitude to books and publishing that could be inspiring and infuriating in equal measure. At my first meeting across the group, a senior editor jolted me by declaring "I love this book so much, I would die to publish it." Dying in order to publish a book seemed extreme. Even in those epic meetings in the Clarendon Building where editors and Delegates made the case for book proposals in front of the Vice-Chancellor, nobody would have thought of making such a personally charged statement. Academic editors obviously took a keen interest in their field, and wanted to publish high-quality content that contributed towards it, but there was not the same kind of emotional attachment to an individual book or its author, although I once heard a medical editor threaten to kill in order to publish a certain book – which seemed to me a much better course of action than dying for it.

This period, from the late 80s to the mid-90s is now regarded as something of a golden age for British literary publishing. It's not obvious that the literature itself has been especially enduring, but it was certainly a lucrative time for a number of writers – and also their agents. These were years of unprecedented advances for literary fiction and, all too often, the publishers were being taken to the cleaners.

At the root of the problem was a mismatch of incentives: editors weren't especially bothered about the size of the advances, because the abiding motivation for them was not to save the company money or even make a particularly good financial deal. Rather, prestige, career progress and industry status came from being able to say that they were Martin Amis's or Salman Rushdie's editor. In fact, a spectacular advance, irrespective of whether it represented good value, was all the more likely to get their name in the media. And this was a time when literary advances, prizes, feuds and rivalries were very much being covered by the papers and magazines, and not just the trade press. A big book launch in London in the early 1990s could be a major cultural event – attended by media and celebrities, and invariably costing the publisher a fortune.

Compounding things, there was also a skills mismatch between the agents and editors. Many of the top literary agents were experienced industry figures and formidable negotiators. The likes of Gillon Aitken, Michael Sissons and Andrew Wylie were steeped in commercial publishing, and far more knowledgeable about ancillary rights, contract law and sales projections than the starstruck editors they were negotiating with. And of course, unlike most of the editors, they had a direct ownership and stake in their agencies, and were determined to get the best deal not just for their clients but also themselves.

In fact, agent-editor 'negotiations' makes it sound more adversarial than it actually was. Editors and agents were usually friends, and had often worked together previously. All too often this led to an unhelpful tendency among some editors to see 'management' as the enemy, and they would readily side with their authors and agents against the company that employed them. In this respect, there was as much a drinking culture as there had been in my previous jobs, but it was very different. It was bars and restaurants in Soho rather than the pub around the corner from the office, and literary editors were more likely to socialize with authors, critics, agents, journalists and editors at other publishing companies rather than direct colleagues. This didn't make management easy – after a big party or launch attended by editors, it was a familiar occurrence to read accounts of new company policies or internal disagreements in the pages of *Private Eye* and the diaries of newspaper columnists.

The lack of commercial nous among literary editors could be stunning – and financially disastrous. In one especially costly case, Secker & Warburg had an author whose paperback rights had been licensed out to Penguin for the previous seven years. A senior editor at Secker renewed this arrangement and proudly reported back that it was for over a million pounds. I looked over the (already signed) contract, and noticed that instead of it being for another seven years it was actually designated as for the duration of copyright. When I queried this, the editor said that the copyright would run out in little more than seven years and so the difference was negligible. In fact, the term of copyright had recently been extended from 50 to 70 years after the death of the author, and so what he had actually done was license the rights to Penguin not for seven but for twenty-seven years. The author in question was George Orwell, whose works eventually entered the public domain in 2021, after selling in the millions around the world. The editor seemed to have been only faintly aware that copyright rules, the legal basis of almost all value in publishing, had changed, never felt it necessary to apologise for his blunder and went on to enjoy a successful career as a literary agent.

One event in particular from these times illustrates the hazards of working with big literary figures. Reed sent couriers over to all of its Methuen authors who were being asked to novate their contracts – essentially to update their contracts, with the same terms and conditions, to the new legal entity. A motorbike courier duly went to her home to get Lady Antonia Fraser's signature, whose acclaimed historical biographies we had been publishing for many years. Unfortunately, the door was answered by her partner, the dramatist Harold Pinter, and in the course of the exchange with the courier an altercation arose. The notoriously short-tempered Pinter became extremely annoyed at what he saw as the impudence of the request. Shortly afterwards, not only did Pinter announce he was moving all of his copyrights from Methuen to Faber, but his great friend, the playwright Simon Gray, wrote to tell us he was doing the same. We never got to the bottom of exactly what happened on Lady Antonia's doorstep, but it proved costly for us and was a lesson in how easily in the literary world one can wreck an author-publisher relationship.

DISTINCTLY NON-LITERARY BESTSELLERS

B ut it was far from just literary publishing. Methuen at the time was the country's leading humour publisher, led by Geoffrey Strachan. As the senior editor at Methuen, he was not only responsible for works by distinguished dramatists, but also the children's list and a hugely successful range of humour titles. In the days before endless repeats of classic sitcoms on cable television, we would publish the scripts to shows such as *Fawlty Towers* and Peter Cook and Dudley Moore sketches. Every year Methuen launched a Christmas list with books produced by the likes of the Monty Pythons, Denis Norden, Frank Muir, Victoria Wood and so on – before videos and DVDs came to dominate, such books were popular gifts. And they were often very good – the comic talent tended to be highly literate and would work with Geoffrey and his team to come up with original concepts and material. In some cases, the authors would move between genres – Methuen published John Cleese's bestselling self-help book *Families and How to Survive Them*. Under Geoffrey's guidance, the playwright Sue Townsend came up with the Adrian Mole series, a 1980s cultural phenomenon, with Townsend going onto to become one of the country's leading comic novelists.

On the children's side, again through Methuen (and some through Heinemann), Reed controlled the publishing rights to some of the best-loved and greatest selling titles and characters including Tintin, Baba the Elephant, Winnie the Pooh, Ant and Bee, and Thomas the Tank Engine. We sold a million copies of Michael Jackson's autobiography *Moonwalk*, although it was widely regarded as unreadable. It was a new kind of publishing for me, one in which brands, marketing and public relations took centre stage.

This was brought home to me when, travelling across the US in the early 1990s, I noticed that a novel called *The Bridges of Madison County* was flying off the shelves, and had been on the New York Times best-seller list for 100 weeks. I came back to London and, on inquiring who was publishing it in the UK, discovered that it was actually us, but that in our wisdom we had changed the title to *Love in Black and White* on the grounds that no one knew where the bridges of Madison County were. The book was selling only moderately well. I pointed out that no one knew where the bridge on the River Kwai was either, wrote a letter of apology to the booksellers and we hastily restored its original title – with an immediate leap in sales.

"Where's there's a hit there's a writ" is an old saying from the music industry, and it was certainly my experience in trade publishing that, the bigger the seller, the more likely the lawyers would have to be called in. This was especially the case when large personalities were involved, and there were few larger in the early 1990s than Robert Maxwell.

In late 1991 we were about to publish the paperback edition of Tom Bower's biography *Maxwell: The Outsider* when the chief of executive of Reed International, Peter Davies, called me. The book had already been out in hardback by a small publisher, but Maxwell was determined that there would be no mass market edition. Having threatened Peter with all manner of legal injunctions, Maxwell played his trump card – if we went ahead and published the biography, he would instruct the British Printing Corporation (which he owned) to immediately stop printing all of IPC's magazines, owned by Reed. This was a significant threat – we were loath to back down in the face of Maxwell's bullying and censorship, but we also knew that if the magazines couldn't be printed then it would result in major disruption, jobs lost and advertising revenues frozen. We postponed the date of publication and wondered what to do. But Maxwell's intimidation worked only for a short time: for while we were still deliberating, he fell off his yacht and resolved the issue for us. We went out with a revised paperback edition shortly after his death, and it inevitably sold tremendously well.

And *Maxwell: The Outsider* was not the only Tom Bower book I was involved in. We agreed to publish his biography of Mohamed Al-Fayed. Fayed, then owner of Harrods and much else, was distinctly unenthusiastic about this project. He invited me to Harrods, asked if I could either stop the book or at least send him the manuscript to vet – in exchange for a gift or two. When I declined, he persistently sent me requests to see the book throughout its production process. It wasn't until the advance copies arrived that I asked a courier to deliver a copy to him with my compliments. The courier returned shortly thereafter still holding the book, and informed me that Mr Al-Fayed had asked him to return it with his compliments and suggested I wipe my arse with the book.

But the bestseller I was most closely involved with was something else entirely. In early 1992, passing through New York for a couple of days, I called in for a catch-up with the then head of Warner Books, the publishing division of the media and entertainment conglomerate, Time-Warner. He was far from happy – that morning, his boss had just announced an enormous $25m dollar deal with the pop star Madonna, encompassing two albums, a video and a book. Much to his dismay, the book component of this contract was $5m, wiping out all of his commissioning budget for the year in one sweep. Partly to help him out, I immediately offered him $1m for the non-US English rights, which he gratefully accepted, although all he could tell me about the book was that it would be called *Sex* and would feature a lot of pictures.

Back in London, the reception to my news was decidedly mixed. The marketing department told me that it was the kind of book that you read with one hand, while both Methuen and Heinemann were resistant to taking it on – they had children's lists and the editors said that they didn't want their brands sullied. So we decided to put it through Secker & Warburg despite their protestations. The book went into production and I went off to the Harvard Business School.

Anxiety only increased as the book went through the editorial and production process, and the nature of its contents began to leak to the media. Thankfully, I was in Boston for most of this, but my mother worried that I would be imprisoned for pornography on my return. Several US printers refused to print *Sex* on the grounds that they were also publishing bibles. Paul Hamlyn was still Chair of Reed and, on one of my visits back to London, he asked me to see him so we could go over the proofs together. We examined the pictures in sombre silence, with his only comment being: "I'm not at all keen on the one with the dog." But there was little that we could do about it by this point.

I was in Boston when my advance copy arrived. The postman at the College rushed over with the book. At the time, I was deeply pre-occupied with the process of trying to put a cricket team together, largely made up of international students. This had been proving difficult at the best of times, and that afternoon practice was abandoned as the whole team collapsed into a scrum to crowd over the book. It was then that I knew that sales, at least, were not going to be a problem.

I travelled down to New York for the launch in the Meatpacking District of Manhattan, which is now extremely fashionable but at the time was still something of a no-go area after dark. As the taxi driver nervously dropped me off, I immediately realized that I had badly misjudged the dress code. I was wearing the preppy gear of a mature business student at Harvard, while almost everyone else was half naked except for leather thongs and metal studs, and the chief accessory was not a briefcase but whips and chains. Models were arranged in tableaus, recreating some of the more explicit photographs from the book. It felt like a long way from the editorial meetings at OUP. Blundering around at some point in the night after having drunk my own bodyweight in champagne, I was introduced to Madonna's head of public relations and we discussed the idea that Madonna might give a talk on marketing at Harvard Business School. Apparently, Madonna herself was taken with the idea. I staggered out at 1am and got the train from Penn Central Station. At this time of night, the station was empty except for hobos and drunkards, but for the first time that entire evening I felt relatively safe. Back at Harvard, I told the head of the programme that Madonna was willing to give a guest lecture on marketing. He was enthusiastic, but felt that he ought to run it past the Dean, who promptly vetoed it, so Madonna never got to give her talk at Harvard Business School. A great pity, as she is universally recognized as one of the greatest marketeers of the last 30 years.

Back in the UK, Reed printed 180,000 copies retailing at £25. It was an immediate sell out. We reprinted another 180,000 two weeks later, which also sold out. Among the gay community especially, it was the must-have Christmas gift that year. The book is regarded as a classic of 1990s pop culture and today a first edition of *Sex* still in its wrapper sells for $1000. Whatever he may have thought of the book, Paul Hamlyn, always an astute investor, made sure he had ten copies. The great shame is that it was actually a two-book deal, but as far as I know a sequel is yet to be produced.

CHAPTER FIVE: CONSOLIDATION, CHANGE AND CONTROVERSIES

The merging of hardback and paperback publishers; the emergence and growth of retail chains; the rapid decline of book clubs; the demise (and legacy) of British theological publishing; battles over the Net Book Agreement; Elsevier comes to the UK and the 'tail of the rat'; the Reed Books fire sale.

THE 'BIG BANG' OF TRADE PUBLISHING

Establishing Mandarin Paperbacks, the task that took up my first years at Reed, was very much part of the industry trend of the time. Up until then, ever since Allen Lane had pioneered the mass market paperback format in the 1930s, almost all trade publishers had tended to license out their paperback rights to other publishers such as Penguin or Pan. In the days before teleordering and online selling, such 'backlist' companies were usually thought to be the only ones able to effectively reach the wider market: they had substantial sales rep forces, greater distribution capacity, marketing expertise and the means to get high volumes of books into newsagents, stations and airports. A common feature in many such outlets would be branded paperback racks and spinners, owned by the likes of Pan or Corgi, well positioned near the counter – sales reps visiting a shop would usually make a point of filling their competitors' spinner with their own offerings. Traditional publishing houses, or 'front list' publishers did not feel confident enough to match this and undertake paperback marketing and sales themselves.

But in the 1980s all this changed – and publishers decided it was time to stop licensing out their biggest assets, especially as they often did it to competitors. Not surprisingly, this didn't always go down well. Many of OUP's key titles had been licensed to Granada publishing, a subsidiary of the Granada media and television conglomerate, but this was now reviewed. We decided to revoke the licensing agreement for one of our most popular titles and publish the paperback version of the *Oxford Children's Dictionary* ourselves when, after the standard seven years, it came up for renewal. Granada Books was run at the time by Alewyn Birch, an exuberant but also rather pugnacious character, who promptly hit the roof and sued OUP.

Fortunately, we were able to settle the matter through arbitration rather than the expense of going to a court of law. Less fortunately, the arbiter's decision was released while Alewyn and I were both attending the International Publishers Association conference in Mexico City in 1984. We were having breakfast in the hotel restaurant when we received the verdict and I had to witness his violent displeasure at first hand. But Alewyn was a brilliant publisher and a few years later, when Reed was setting up Mandarin, we hired him as a consultant to advise us.

It is understandable why Alewyn had been so upset at the time – precedents such as this heralded an existential threat. As more originating publishers adopted the same strategy, paperback, or 'backlist publishers' now risked going out of business as their pipeline of titles disappeared. It explains why, when Peter Mayer was chief executive of Penguin, his response was to acquire hardback publishers such as Hamish Hamilton and Michael Joseph and so build up what was called at the time a 'vertical' publishing company, with hardback and paperback imprints all under the same roof. It has been likened to the publishing industry's version of the City's 'big bang' happening at the same time and which saw similar consolidation. What had previously been separate financial services companies, with different market roles, were now merging or acquiring one another. Within just a few years the distinction between front list and backlist publishers had almost entirely disappeared and since the 1990s books have been released in hardback (or at least trade paperback) and then migrate a year later to the same publisher's cheaper paperback format. Apart from translation rights and the licensing out of specialist formats, for instance large-type versions for the partially sighted, this is how most trade publishing is structured.

One of the under-appreciated consequences of this is that authors have financially benefited. Under the traditional arrangement, a paperback publisher would pay an advance to the front list publisher and then the standard royalty, which would be equally split 50/50 between the original publisher and author. But from this point on, publishers would just maintain their existing royalty agreements, paying out the same rate (usually between 5% and 10% of the cover price) to the author irrespective of the format and so, in effect, doubling what the paperback royalty rate had been.

THE CHANGING RETAIL LANDSCAPE

The changes and consolidation among publishing companies was a reflection, and also a response, to changes in bookselling at the time.

Working in a bookshop has long been a traditional entry point into publishing, but unlike many of my peers I never worked in bookselling even as a student. In my first job at Harrap, though, it was soon made clear to me how book publishing and selling were intertwined. From our office in Holborn, we were within close proximity to what was one of the world's great centres of bookselling, and we needed to be. Every day shop managers would come to our warehouse on the ground floor and order their books. This just seemed to be how things were: Charing Cross Road had been synonymous with bookshops ever since the Foyle brothers and others had opened their stores there at the beginning of the twentieth century, and it was an internationally renowned destination for book lovers.

But all of this would change. The first Waterstone's opened on Old Brompton Road in 1982. In line with Tim Waterstone's strategy, it was in a slightly more run-down, and cheaper, location than the area's premier retail street – in this case the King's Road, and would help to raise the profile of the neighbourhood. Tim Waterstone deserves a lot of credit (and some opprobrium from independent booksellers) for transforming bookselling, but it was a wider trend, with the launch and expansion of a number of high-quality national book chains. Pentos bought Dillons, and they would often be in direct competition with Waterstone's, while Ottakar's also started, with a particularly good range of children's books. Meanwhile, Blackwell's was building up its network of stores on university campuses and towns, and Books Etc was establishing itself as an independent before its sale to the multinational Borders Group, which had grown rapidly across US college towns since the 1970s. After many years in which the choice had either been small, family-owned bookshops or else WH Smith (where Tim Waterstone had started out) these chains were a revelation – well stocked, thoughtfully designed and, at least to begin with, staffed by young men and women who were themselves enthusiastic and knowledgeable readers. At their best, they were able to provide the intimacy and pleasure of a good independent bookshop, along with the service associated with a well-managed retail corporation. In turn, growth was spurred by heightened media coverage and interest in literary authors such as the likes of Martin Amis, Rose Tremain, Julian Barnes and William Boyd with broadsheet newspapers launching review supplements and needing copy to fill them.

Following in the wake of the national book chains came the supermarkets. As they steadily ate up more and more of the retail market, expanding from groceries into clothing, domestic appliances and home furnishings, it was inevitable that books would come into their sights. After starting out with cookery and interior design, they moved into general trade, children's books and fiction – by 2007, when the last of the Harry Potter series was released, supermarkets were ordering half a million copies, and drastically under-cutting the bookshops. In 2011 things had got to the point that *The Bookseller* gave the award for 'chain bookseller of the year' to Sainsbury's.

Given this, it is easier to understand why trade publishing also radically changed. The days when a publisher like Harrap felt that it needed to be located close to London's principal bookselling cluster were gone – by the 1990s, Waterstone's had more than 200 outlets across the UK. Gone too, was the need for a large network of sales reps to travel up and down the country, visiting each town's bookshop and taking their orders. Centralised teleordering and stock management systems meant not just efficiencies, but a very different way of interacting with booksellers. While it is heartening that the number of independent bookshops has risen in the last few years, the bigger truth is that it comes after more than twenty years of continuous decline. For a publishing company now, more important than regional sales reps is to have negotiated good terms of trade with wholesalers, built an efficient storage and distribution system and developed working relations with the management at Waterstone's and the supermarkets – not to mention Amazon.

In the face of pressure from supermarkets and then Amazon, the speed of high street consolidation only increased. When I was Chair of the Publishers Association in the mid-2000s, Waterstone's made a bid to take over Ottakar's and we unsuccessfully objected to the deal through the Competition Commission (now the Competition and Markets Authority). We always knew we had little hope of success. In order to make the case that there is a risk of injurious market domination, you need to have a precise and tightly defined definition of the sector in question. If it had just been dedicated high street booksellers then we might possibly have had a winnable case, but in the modern retail landscape, it is a sector that encompasses far bigger players – the supermarkets and of course, Amazon which takes something like 50% of all print book sales in the UK. In this context, it was judged that the incorporation of Ottakar's stores into the Waterstone's group would have little impact on consumers and that it would "not result in a substantial lessening of competition". Nor is it any great surprise that, by the end 2022, Waterstone's had acquired Foyles's eight and Blackwell's eighteen bookshops. The regulators have shown no interest, and the response from publishers and booksellers alike has been little more than a shrug of the shoulders as Waterstone's applies its terms of trade to these acquisitions, thus reducing further the share of a book's revenue accruing to author and publisher.

THE DEMISE OF BOOK CLUBS

The ups and downs of book shops and the struggles they have faced in the internet age are well documented and newspapers continue to cover their prospects. Less well known is the story of book clubs and mail order sales, and their dramatic decline in the 1990s. But for many years, such clubs had been an important part of the bookselling landscape: a means of buying books wherever you lived, a route for undiscovered authors and a way for books to find their market. Many authors enjoyed highly successful careers, not least Wilbur Smith, through the profile they steadily built up through book clubs.

Most prominent among these was Book Club Associates, a joint venture founded by Doubleday (and later taken over by Bertelsmann) and WH Smith in the 1960s. BCA came to dominate the market, less with its own brand but through more than twenty mass-market and thematic book clubs, ranging from World Books, The Literary Guild and Book of the Month Club to science fiction, military history, cricket and other genres. In the early 1990s WH Smith sold its stake to Reed International for about £50million and as I had been part of the due diligence team, I was one of Reed's representatives on the BCA board. It wasn't long afterwards that it began its descent, although in fairness I couldn't be held entirely responsible.

As with other book clubs, many of which had long histories, the business model was to sign up customers as members of a bookselling syndicate, allowing them to get books at substantially reduced prices compared to standard book shops. In exchange for these reduced prices, members were obliged to purchase a minimum number of books each year. In subscribing to a book club and committing to a certain number of titles, people were members rather than customers, and the club was not subject to the Net Book Agreement which required that books could not be sold for less than their cover price.

Book clubs like this tended to work on a low price and high sales volumes model, and these volumes could be very high indeed. At its peak in the 1980s, the BCA had a mailing list of four million individuals, with two and a half million active members. Sales were well above £100 million with a healthy margin. But it was a relentless business, and depended on constantly driving up membership. This was done almost entirely by advertising in the supplements and back pages of Sunday broadsheet newspapers, principally the Sunday Times. The adverts contained a small coupon that you had to cut out, fill in and send back. By midday on the following Monday the marketing manager already had a very good idea of how successful the advert had been and how many new members had been acquired. It was reckoned that signing up a new member would cost £50 and the rule of the thumb was that they would earn you a £100 profit provided they stayed for at least two years. The great marketing insight we gleaned in my time there was that response dramatically decreased when we dropped the little scissors icon and dotted line around the coupon. The best titles for recruiting members were either safe bets, such as reference books, or slightly titillating titles, such as *The Joy of Sex*, which people would rather buy through the mail than in person.

As a joint venture, the chairmanship of BCA rotated between Bertelsmann and Reed. This was far from an easy relationship, and there were significant differences in management style. The lowest point came when Manfred Herriger, Bertelsmann's representative and the then chair, wanted to sack the CEO Graham Williams, who was, I thought, doing a perfectly good job. I was deputy chairman at the time, and Herriger asked if I could invite Graham to my office in London, so he could meet with him. Herriger duly travelled to London for the meeting, only to tell me 10 minutes beforehand that he didn't think his English was good enough to explain to Graham that he was going to be fired, and so could I do it. A talented publisher and marketing executive, Graham would go on to run Panini stickers.

BCA's revenues peaked at something close to £150m in 1993, but this wouldn't last much longer, for the demise of the Net Book Agreement undermined the business model of book clubs. Many people in trade publishing had thought that this wouldn't happen, and that even without the regulatory advantage over retailers, book clubs and mail order catalogues would remain a durable way of building up loyal customers and getting books to those parts of the country that weren't within easy reach of a bookshop. But it wasn't to be, and membership went into continuous decline until the launch of Amazon in the UK in the late nineties killed off the model for good. BCA went through a number of corporate sales and restructures before folding in the 2000s.

In the UK, book clubs still exist today, but they are small and tend to be specialist affairs. Members sign up to subscription boxes not to be able to buy cheap books, but rather to receive books that have been chosen as part of a curated offer, and for certain genres, such as fantasy, they can still drive sales. The last successful and genuinely mass-market book club was a venture called The Book People. Founded by Ted Smart, who began by driving around Surrey with a van full of books, this had a different model – he visited offices and other workplaces, selling books directly to employees. By 1990, there were more than a hundred Book People local distributors around the country visiting workplaces such as banks, schools and hospitals.

In the early nineties, I brought together Ted Smart and Herriger, the then Chair of BCA, for a lunch meeting, to see if there was any scope for working together. Herriger was dismissive – at the time, the Book People had a turnover of around ten million pounds, a fraction of BCA. As is the way of these things, within just a few years, Book People's revenues were higher than BCA. But they too found themselves struggling to compete with the likes of Amazon, and moved into online bookselling before going into administration.

THE DECLINE OF THEOLOGICAL PUBLISHING

A common claim is that the Bible is the best-selling book of all time. Reed may have sold hundreds of thousands of copies of Madonna's *Sex*, but it has been estimated that anything over five billion Bibles have been printed. Almost as soon as William Caxton brought the first printing press to England in the 1470s, people started to produce Bibles and it is certainly the case that Bibles, and religious texts in general, were for centuries the mainstay of the British publishing industry.

The fact that this is no longer the case isn't always fully appreciated. Looking back on the last half century, it is easy to focus on what have been the most obvious areas of growth: scientific publishing, English language teaching, children's literature and coffee table picture books. But it is better thought of as a series of pivots, with publishers advancing into certain areas as others have declined and probably the greatest of these has been the UK's shift from being an international centre of theological publishing to English language teaching.

At OUP in the 1980s, Bibles and prayer books were still quite profitable, although it was really more a case of printing rather than publishing. Requiring little in the way of editorial oversight, the emphasis was on supplying churches with a variety of formats and covers – this involved different materials as well as colours, and gold and silver gilt edges (a good example of product diversification). Within the UK, these sales were steadily falling as church attendance inexorably declined in the late twentieth century. But this wasn't the case everywhere: OUP's Scofield Reference Bible, originally published in 1909 and with annotations by the fundamentalist theologian Cyrus Scofield, was seeing increased sales in many parts of the world, as more evangelical strains of Christianity took hold.

On condition of being the publisher of the King James, or authorized, Bible, OUP had for centuries had certain responsibilities, to safeguard it from piracy. This meant that once a year there was a coming together of the 'protectors of the copyright of the Bible' at Westminster Abbey, in which I would have to represent OUP. The morning-long meeting was attended by various bishops, theologians and senior clergy, and would always begin with prayers for God to help us make good decisions. While I was there, the principal topic of discussion was related to updates to the New English Bible, which a committee of Church scholars had put together in 1960s, so that it might be more accessible to a modern readership. These deliberations were not exactly speedy – after all, it had taken almost four hundred years for them to come up with the official revision to the King James edition. For all I know, I might still be one of the protectors.

At Reed in the 1990s, there were still a few ways to make money from publishing Bibles. Paul Hamlyn himself had proven this not long before, when he cooked up a deal with George Weidenfeld and Marcus Sieff to sell the Bible in Marks and Spencer stores. The irony that the New Testament was being brought to Britain's mass market by three Jews was not lost on them. Through Hamlyn's various other acquisitions, we had also inadvertently found ourselves owning a Bible publisher in the shape of the 'Queen's Printer' – Eyre and Spottiswoode, the venerable London-based printer, founded in the 18th century, and which had merged with Methuen in the 1970s. Eyre Methuen, as it was briefly known, possessed a perpetual copyright to the King James Bible (in England but not Scotland), along with OUP and Cambridge University Press. Notwithstanding the standardisation of international intellectual property rules, perpetual copyright remains a quirk. Another, better known, one is the specific legislation which grants Great Ormond Street Hospital an everlasting right to royalties from J.M. Barrie's *Peter Pan*. No one at Reed was much interested in any of this, and so we looked to sell our publishing rights to the King James Bible to either of the two obvious bidders. We ran a blind auction and it was a memorable morning in the office when the offers arrived over the fax machine – first of all, a very respectable £100,000 from OUP. We crouched around the machine and watched, to our surprise and joy as CUP's bid came through an hour later, the machine laboriously printing out the astonishing figure of £900,000. The only snag was that CUP demanded the King's Seal that accompanied this, which prompted panic and a week of frenetic searching, before eventually turning it up in the basement of a lawyer's office.

It is highly unlikely that anyone would be offering such sums of money for Bible publishing rights, even perpetual ones, today. While numerous small ecclesiastical presses still operate around the country, they tend to be family businesses catering for local markets and faith groups. In North America, by contrast, with its heightened levels of religiosity and evangelical Christianity, religious publishing remains big business. Over the last twenty years, HarperCollins Christian Publishing has bought a number of companies and built up a group of imprints under the Zondervan brand with an annual turnover of well over $100m.

But the role of theological publishing in shaping the British industry today should not be overlooked. It is not just OUP and CUP whose history is bound up with the publishing and printing of religious works. The origins of HarperCollins lie in part with William Collins, a Presbyterian school master, who founded the company in Glasgow in 1819 to publish hymn and prayer books, and whose success was largely based on obtaining the licence to publish the Bible in Scotland. More generally, the enormous global expansion over the last fifty years in the publishing of English language teaching was in large part based on the companies, offices and trade networks that had originally been built by the UK's religious publishers.

THE END OF THE NET BOOK AGREEMENT

In the early 1990s, the European Union enacted the Copyright Duration Directive, which harmonised intellectual property rights across all EU member states and determined that copyright would apply for 70 years from the death of the author, regardless of when the work was published. This replaced the previous 50-year term that had been in place in the UK and many other countries, in line with the Berne Convention of 1886. This was all decided at the European level and while it was something welcomed by publishers and authors and championed by trade associations, it was not something that many in the industry had argued about or even discussed much, despite its hugely beneficial impact on asset values of copyrights and thus publishers.

It was a very different matter with the other great regulatory change of the last fifty years: the end of the retail price maintenance for books, known as the Net Book Agreement (NBA). This was an issue that bitterly divided the industry in the 1990s and was a major pre-occupation during my time at Reed. This long-standing arrangement between the Publishers Association and booksellers, which dated back to 1900, had meant that all books published in the UK could not be sold below the 'cover price' – the price fixed by the publisher. Any bookseller who tried to sell a book for less than this would be in breach.

The NBA had been challenged and tested over the course of the twentieth century. In the 1960s, the Restrictive Practices Court conducted an inquiry but ruled that it should remain, on the grounds that high margins from best-selling books enabled publishers to also publish works of merit by less widely read authors. It was, however, agreed that there could be a week in January when booksellers were allowed to sell off unsold stock at sale prices, and textbooks could be declared non-net by the publisher and then sold at a discount directly to schools. Second hand books were exempt from the NBA, and there were provisions for discounts to libraries, and of course there were book clubs which ingeniously circumnavigated the rules by building up a membership who paid a subscription in order to select discounted books, rather than actually purchasing them individually. Imported books were not subject to the NBA's jurisdiction.

Despite all of these cracks in the system, the NBA was still in place and did not finally succumb until the early 1990s. The Conservative governments of the 1980s had disliked the NBA and saw it as the kind of protectionist regulation they were ideologically averse to, but it is worth saying that Paul Hamlyn, by no means a Conservative, was also opposed to the NBA on the grounds that it made retailers lazy and held back innovation in bookselling. My objections to it were more pragmatic, for it had become clear to me people were increasingly finding ways to get round it and that it would be impossible to maintain in the radically shifting retail landscape. Large bookshop chains were spreading, while supermarkets were also moving into bookselling, and if UK publishers were insisting on a fixed cover price, then these retailers had the clout to import in volume from American publishers who were not subject to the NBA, and thus able to sell books at a price advantage to smaller booksellers. But this was still a minority view in the industry – most publishers were vehemently opposed to scrapping it, while independent booksellers had come to value the protection it gave them.

Things came to a head as the Dillons book chain, part of Terry Maher's Pentos retail group, expanded rapidly from its base in London, with more than a hundred stores across the country. A strident critic of the NBA, Maher had publicly campaigned for its abolition for years and now, running the country's largest book chain, he saw his chance to dismantle it. In 1989 Maher declared that Dillons would sell that year's six Booker Prize shortlisted novels at a substantial discount. The autumn announcement of the Booker shortlist is one of British fiction's annual highlights and a major media event. It was an obvious, high-profile act of provocation by Maher, and one which immediately put publishers and other booksellers in a quandary.

Across our publishing companies, Reed had two of the books on that year's shortlist, and we were prepared for this. As a precaution, we had already updated our computerized sales systems, so that all of our titles could be sold as 'non-net'. And so, much to the annoyance of the Publishers Association, we went along with Dillons and supplied them with books in the knowledge that they would be sold below the cover price. As the books were all non-net we were not obliged to cease supply of those titles.

Just as Maher had intended, the NBA was now fatally weakened. Tim Hely Hutchinson, chief executive of Hodder, was eager to sell his leading titles at discount in order to build up market share for mass-market paperbacks, and similarly let it be known that he would provide books to Dillons whatever the sale price. As a result of all this, Reed did briefly leave the Publishers Association, but given that Reed International's assorted companies made up at least ten percent of their membership revenues, it wasn't too long before an accommodation was reached. Many of the booksellers were similarly cross. Toby Blackwell, head of the famous bookselling family, was so angry that he wanted to ban the sale of Reed's books from the flagship Blackwell's bookshop in Oxford. This was possibly illegal, so instead they decided to make it as difficult as possible to buy our top titles. Much of the ire was directed towards *The Jolly Christmas Postman*, a children's picture book by Janet and Allan Ahlberg, based on their much-loved Jolly Postman series, which had been specially commissioned for the 1991 Christmas market. Instead of being placed near the sales counter, the book was consigned to the very top shelf at the rear of the children's section. But the only real consequence of this was that it hit their sales, while the poor bookshop assistants had to go all the way to the back of the shop and climb up a ladder every time someone asked for a copy.

Within a year, the Director General of the Office of Fair Trading had called for a review of the NBA and, following on from this, the Restrictive Practices Court overturned the 1962 ruling, declaring that it no longer served the public interest. The view now was that the abolition of the NBA meant that book prices would potentially be lower for consumers and this was sufficient to over-ride other considerations. For all the grumbling from many of its members, the Publishers Association was unwilling to take any further action. But this wasn't the end of it, for the defence of the NBA was then taken up by John Calder, an independent publisher of considerable inherited wealth who had made a name for himself in the 1960s hosting arts salons and publishing some of the leading figures of European avant-garde literature. Calder had denounced the Publishers Association as 'suicidal' for failing to fight against the OFT, and took it upon himself to single-handedly challenge the ruling.

So it was that I was duly summoned to the Courts of Justice as a witness in Calder's quixotic attempt to reverse what had now been accepted by government and most of the industry. Being examined in court is rarely an enjoyable experience, but as soon as the questioning began, my anxieties dissipated. Any sound arguments for maintaining the NBA certainly weren't made in the court that day. Making the case himself, without a barrister, Calder deployed a series of eccentric arguments – he began by bringing it to the judge's attention that I had studied science at university instead of humanities, and so could not possibly be a fit and proper publisher. He went on to point out that in New York City the homicide rate was three times higher than London, and that this could be attributed to the US never having had the equivalent of the NBA. The judge seemed to have even less patience for him than I did and the ruling was upheld.

These battles were all fought in the 1990s and, of course, what no one foresaw was how the internet would shortly come to transform bookselling along with all other forms of retail. Certainly, the argument propounded by Maher that the abolition of the NBA would lead to a flourishing in bookselling was misplaced – there are now far fewer independent bookshops than previously. Similarly, the great hope of many publishers was that it would bring about a reduction in returned books, and that shops would sell unsold stock at lower prices rather than go to the troubling of sending them back, but alas the level of returns seems to be as high as ever. But it should also be said many of the dire warnings voiced at the time have never come to pass – the number of titles published in the UK has only increased since the demise of the NBA, as has the total number of books sold.

If the NBA had been in place, it's quite possible that Amazon would never have been able to discount so aggressively and dominate the British market in the same way. It is also often pointed out that in France, Germany and other parts of Europe they still have an equivalent of the NBA, and this is often held as a reason why so many bookshops can still be found in the centre of Paris and other cities. A difference often overlooked, however, is that they have the natural protection of being non-English speaking, and so stores cannot easily be filled with American imports. One problem for British publishers and small bookshops was that the US never had the NBA, and so larger retailers could always import books from America at a lower price. When *Harry Potter and the Deathly Hallows* went on sale, supermarket chains such as Asda ordered half a million copies and sold them for less than Bloomsbury's recommended retail price of £17.99. If Bloomsbury had refused to supply the books, then Asda would happily have imported them from the US via a European intermediary.

And so, a quarter of a century since the demise of the NBA, the consequences on book publishing and selling remain hard to judge. Disagreements on the issue may no longer be bitter, but they still remain and James Daunt has reduced discounted pricing at Waterstone's. Yet no one since John Calder has made an attempt to challenge this in the courts, and it seems highly unlikely to ever come back. Although Nigel Newton, the chief executive of Bloomsbury Publishing, has certainly made his thoughts plain, more than once exclaiming to me: "Why the hell did you ever get rid of the margin-protecting agreement?!"

REED ELSEVIER: THE ANTI-BOOK PUBLISHER

In the middle of the night in late October 1992, in my student digs at the Harvard Business School in Boston, I got a call from Ian Irvine, prompting me to fall out of my narrow bed. Ian told me that Reed International had agreed to merge with Elsevier, and that it was going to be announced to the stock exchange the next morning. Having been on a university campus for months, I had had no idea this was coming and it was an unpleasant surprise. It wasn't a share swap or a corporate agreement – it was a full-blown merger, and things were going to be very different. I climbed back into bed and, although I had overcome my surprise, I was full of foreboding.

From the beginning the signs weren't good. Elsevier had wanted to merge with Reed in order to fulfil its long-standing global ambitions. Anxious to be much more than a Dutch company, it had already acquired Pergamon from Maxwell and attempted a merger with Pearson. When the Pearson deal collapsed, the executives turned their attention to Reed. The chair of the newly-minted Reed Elsevier, Pierre Vinken, was something of a corporate superstar in the Netherlands, often photographed with Dutch starlets, but he had risen up through scientific journal publishing and had reportedly told Peter Mayer, the then chief executive of Penguin that he hated books. Given that I had recently taken charge of Reed International Books, I was not optimistic about my prospects under him.

This was soon confirmed in the first board meeting I attended. Pierre Vinken and Peter Davies were in theory the co-chairs of the new business, but Peter actually sat at another table and said nothing. Before moving into scientific publishing, Vinken had been an academic neuroscientist and he drew a picture of a rat and explained how all publishing businesses share the same essential anatomy. They have a bright shiny nose and curious whiskers, and a fairly useless tail. Books, he went on to tell us, are the tail of this business. I sat in silence, trying to come up with the best anagrams I could from Reed Elsevier – Vile Deliverers admittedly wasn't a perfect anagram, but felt about right.

It was more than just Vinken – his hostility towards the books sector reflected a deeper suspicion on the part of Elsevier as a whole. With a history dating all the way back to the 16th century Netherlands and originally dedicated to classical studies, it had never moved far from its scholarly roots and puritan ethos. By the late twentieth century, despite having grown into a major corporation, the management still distrusted trade books, and were far more comfortable with academic publishing, science and medicine, research journals and the education market. Although it had always been a publisher, Elsevier's managers brought with them more of the sensibility of an engineering or manufacturing firm. It wasn't like working for any other publisher I had known – there was a relentless focus on hitting the profit growth target. It was also much more white, male and monocultural – every executive was a Dutch man usually well over six foot tall, whereas Reed's workforce now had women in many senior roles, especially editorial, and a much more global profile.

Although he had come from the Reed side, there wasn't much comfort to be had from my new boss, John Mellon. He had been running IPC and brought with him the culture of consumer magazine publishing where the mantra had been to never trust your editors, and to micromanage as much as possible. It was soon made clear to me that my job would be simultaneously to manage the trade books business (the tail of the rat!) as best as I could, while also trying to sell it off. From my perspective, the entire books business (split across consumer, education and academic divisions) was working well together – I had spent much of the last six years trying to build it up and felt that a good management team and structure were in place. We had gone through the painful process of improving distribution and sales teams. We had integrated our back-end and finance systems, including the dreaded royalty payments, and even the software was now working. From a distance, it might have made sense to Elsevier's strategists to rip out consumer books, but not to me nor anyone else that was actually running things.

My first response was to try and do a management buy-out. I went to see Paul Hamlyn who was interested in principle, and then the accountants Pricewaterhouse (now PWC), who promised to bring together a pool of backers. We managed to put together an offer of £400m for what had been Reed International Books, but John Mellon rejected it out of hand. Determined to become a major international academic and B2B player, they were only willing to sell the consumer publishing interests. I knew that I wouldn't be able to make that work – trade, education and academic books all had to be together to make for a viable and financially secure publishing company at the scale we were.

And so I was instructed to continue with overseeing the sale. In my fifty-year career, I have never been further removed from actual publishing than I was at this time. Although technically I was still in charge of Reed International Books, I had to relocate from Michelin House to the company's corporate HQ at Chesterfield Gardens. There were no editors or publishers here, and certainly no books. Rather I shared the offices with the company chauffeurs, accountants, human resources department and the team responsible for managing the company pension. It was here I learnt the interesting fact that, because the pension scheme was obliged to keep a balanced portfolio across sectors and also were unable to use staff pensions to buy stock in our own company (due to regulations brought in after Maxwell's disaster), we had bought heavily in Pearson, and were thus keeping up the share price of our biggest competitor.

It was a gloomy time. Goldman Sachs had been appointed to work with me on the sale and while they undertook the financial projections and market analytics, it was my job to provide the colour and industry know-how, and to pitch the company to a suitable buyer. It was a good team – led by Richard Sharp, who since went on to become the chair of the BBC, and who took a keen interest in the project. It has tended to be my experience with investment bankers that they find publishing a far more absorbing sector than their own. But in truth, my heart was no longer it. There had been a large bonus scheme put in place in order to incentivize us to make a good sale, and if we had been able to sell consumer books I would have been in line for a windfall, but it wasn't enough. Once the possibility of a management buy-out had been dismissed, I knew I would have no long-term future with the company.

In the end, despite the best efforts of Goldman Sachs, we couldn't find a suitable buyer for books, and so Reed Elsevier started the process of carving it up. It soon descended into a fire sale – the myriad publishing houses and ventures that Hamlyn had acquired, and which we had worked so hard to integrate, were broken up and disposed of with brutal speed. Most of the children's division went to Egmont, taking with them Thomas the Tank Engine, Tintin and much else. A management buy-out was negotiated for Hamlyn's beloved illustrated, design and cookery imprints such as Mitchell Beazley, Conran Octopus and Bounty Books, all of which were housed under the new Octopus Publishing Group (now part of the Hachette Group), led by Reed executives and financed by Kleinwort Benson. But it was Random House who probably did the best from all this, spending less than £20 million and ending up with numerous best-sellers and many of English literature's crown jewels: Evelyn Waugh, J.D.Salinger, Steinbeck, *To Kill a Mockingbird*, Bill Bryson, Adrian Mole, Roddy Doyle, Louiis de Bernieres, Graham Greene and much else besides.

It was inevitably messy. The trade books had to be renamed William Heinemann, so that they could be legally differentiated from Heinemann Young Books, now owned by Egmont, and Heinemann Education which remained with Reed Elsevier. I was isolated, the management team I had built was gone and, amidst the carnage, I wanted out. Peter Davies was marginalized, Paul Hamlyn was still a shareholder, but he dedicated his time to the arts and philanthropy and no longer took an active interest in the business. John Mellon was probably the least helpful manager I've ever had, while Ian Irvine might have had personal misgivings about the strategy, but he accepted that a corporate decision had been made and needed to be seen through.

Resigning from Reed Elsevier would not be as awkward as at OUP, but in the corporate world it still wouldn't be straightforward, and it took a while to come to terms. John Mellon showed more interest in me than he had ever done before, and insisted that in order for me to be able to leave, there had to be a comprehensive non-compete agreement in place. The initial one he put forward prevented me from working for any competitor of Reed Elsevier in any market in the world. I naturally refused this, and we wrangled back and forth until I eventually signed a contract that prohibited me from joining any rival in the book market. On hearing this, Ian Irvine groaned and told Mellon that "the last thing Richard wants to do next is books". He was right. I had other plans.

CHAPTER SIX: THE START-UP YEARS

The genius that is Vitek Tracz; outsourcing the R&D; running a publishing start-up; how to sell a publishing business; the multimedia CD-ROM boom; smart uses of technology; the inexorable rise of scientific journal publishing.

I first met Vitek Tracz at the Frankfurt Book Fair in 1983, where he was a highly entertaining presence. He had recently set up a business with Tim Hailstone – Gower Medical, publishing large-format, high-quality medical colour atlases and slide sets. He was there to sell copies in as many languages as possible, and to make sure he had a good time doing it. I was at OUP and though I never dealt with him directly, we soon became friends and stayed in touch throughout my time at Reed.

Vitek, once described by the editor of the BMJ as the 'Picasso of science publishing' is one of the great publishers of my time. He had been born and raised in Poland, where his grandfather had been a travelling mohel, or official circumciser and left to study mathematics in Israel, where he became more interested in cinema and dabbled in feature film production before moving to London in the 1960s to teach film studies. After having failed to turn a profit producing a critically successful Hebrew language feature film, he realised there was money to be made in medical training films – particularly if they were financed by pharmaceutical companies. In a few years he had built up and sold this business, in the course of which his interests had turned to scientific publishing, leading him to set up Gower Medical.

An insatiable entrepreneur and deal maker, Vitek was (and still is) perpetually fascinated by new technologies, with a kind of genius for seeing how they could be used in business and publishing. He could never understand why anyone would ever get into trade publishing despite his own love and understanding of literature– what interested him was technology, the market opportunity, means of delivery and the revenue model. In this, and many other respects, he had a quite different outlook from most publishers. Nor did he have the appearance of a modern media executive. Despite spending large amounts of money on clothes he always looked, as one colleague observed, like a Polish peasant. On one famous occasion, while waiting in the lobby of a law firm to sign the contracts on a deal, a security guard made repeated attempts to eject him, and could not be persuaded that he was in fact a highly valued client rather than an itinerant who had wandered in off the street.

In my last months at Reed Elsevier, I had no firm plans other than going into business with Vitek, and so I went to become chief executive of Current Science Group, where Vitek was founder and chair. While I didn't share Vitek's disdain for trade publishing, I had learnt some things from my time at Reed. One of them was that that, across all of their varied interests, the most commercially successful were the ones with the shortest value chains. Selling directly to librarians or legal practices was much more profitable than selling to bookshops, which meant steep discounts and large returns. Another maxim was that it always better to be in a business in which people had to, rather than wanted to, buy what you were selling.

I also had a good idea of what was happening in journal publishing. Although I had been running books at Reed, following the merger I had made a point of attending the journal strategy meetings and kept an interest – after all, some of Elsevier's most profitable journals were ones I'd worked on back at Pergamon in the 1970s. In particular, I had been in a meeting when the five-year plan was presented to senior management. By this point, Reed Elsevier was by far the world's largest STM publisher. Not only had Elsevier been successfully doing this for more than a century, it had acquired Pergamon's journals and also now, following the merger, had control over the Butterworth-Heinemann journals that had been owned by Reed. In the course of presenting the plan, the Elsevier corporate strategists explained that the projected attrition rate of journal subscribers would be between 1-6 per cent, as university departments and libraries consolidated and created subscription consortia. It tells you much about the mindset of the Elsevier strategists that any unexpected increase in journal subscribers was described not as growth but rather 'negative attrition'. They went on to show that journal prices could rise to match the falling subscribers, and ensure that profits would be maintained – in fact, according to their calculations, we would continue to meet the expected 15% annual rate of profit increase, in line with the overall corporate target. When I asked what would happen if the attrition rate transpired to be 10% or more, I was told that this hadn't been considered as otherwise the model wouldn't work.

It was clear to me that Reed Elsevier was less prepared than they ought to be for the forces that were about to transform academic publishing. The company was far from alone in this, but given the number of corporate strategists they were employing, they had less excuse than most. It was the mid-1990s, the web had been invented five years previously and by every metric, from number of sites to users to time spent online, the internet was experiencing explosive growth. There would be plenty of disruption and things to worry about, and many long-standing features of the publishing landscape were at risk. But there were also huge opportunities for 'negative attrition'. I was still in touch with science publishers in Oxford and at the PA Council and knew that many people, Vitek foremost among them, were thinking imaginatively about technology, business models and new ways of doing publishing. It was a classic case of corporate complacency and fear of change – Reed Elsevier was committed to an extension of the status quo that had worked so well for so long.

Vitek liked to see Current Science as being an outsourced 'R&D department' to the established publishers. He could provide the new thinking and innovation that was harder to do from within an organisation, and he would take the early risks that they wouldn't do themselves. As soon as I arrived at Current Science I could see that there were plenty of options and new ideas out there for us to pursue. By this point Vitek had already built and sold numerous businesses, but there was still a variety of publishing assets, patents and ventures that he was building and which we felt had good potential.

The basis of these were 'current opinions' or review journals which, instead of publishing new research, presented reviews, analysis and surveys of the field. The market opportunity spotted by Vitek was much in line with what Maxwell had foreseen in the 1970s: as the volume of life sciences research and accompanying papers continued to increase, scientists would struggle to stay abreast of everything that was going on.

There was a need for forums and review journals that could synthesise, summarise and assess the relevance of the latest findings.

There were four or five different ventures that did just this, including *Current Biology*, *Current Drugs* and *Current Medicine*. There was also a video database of distinguished scientists, who were interviewed about their life and career, so that their stories would be available to future generations – and so, as Vitek hoped, we could sell extracts for obituaries and archives. We developed *Law City*, which was intended to aggregate and sell law information, and to take on the major legal publishers. There was even a small printing company that was using the latest digital technology to do specialist jobs for local advertisers.

Vitek had also developed something called BioMedNet, which was probably the most innovative and interesting of his ventures. It was intended as a social network for life scientists, although that term wouldn't come into use until much later. The major science publishers at the time were trying to build their own platforms, such as Elsevier's ScienceDirect, but these were principally a means of selling online subscriptions. While BioMedNet did sell individual scientific papers, rather than whole journals, it was intended to be more than this – an online environment for academics and researchers which could become a part of their working lives. It provided a chat room and some knowledge sharing tools, and people could register and have a BioMedNet email address. The technology was quite primitive by today's standards, but this was a full decade before the likes of Facebook or LinkedIn launched, and it was driven by the same insight – to build an online community, in this case life scientists, who could make professional connections, interact and collaborate.

At any one time, there were up to a hundred people working at Current Science and at five or six different business ventures, each one with its own managing director who had a stake in the business. The idea always was to build and in due course sell the ventures – usually to established publishers who would then assimilate, mismanage and eventually dismantle them. Everyone knew that, if successful, the business would be sold at some point, in which case there was a high chance of them losing their jobs. But they also knew that Vitek could be relied upon to rehire them.

Compared to the other companies I had worked in, there were high levels of trust. It helped that so many had a stake in the business, and that we were funded through earnings and previous sales, so we never had to deal with external investors. It also helped that we had Andrew Crompton, who was Vitek's consigliere and did a brilliant job in managing much of the operation. But it also had something to do with Vitek's distinctive recruitment strategy. One of his management principles was that he was a strong believer in personal relationships, in fact outright nepotism, as a means of organising a company. He would often hire someone from, say Turkey or the Czech Republic, and then if they were any good encourage them to get their friends and relations to join. The result was that the company felt like a large extended family.

Our offices were at Middlesex House, Fitzrovia. It wasn't a traditional location for a publishing business, but the geography of London publishing was changing and practicality trumped image when it came to offices. There was no more Bibendum restaurant and wine bar on the ground floor, no extravagant expense accounts or company cars – and certainly no drivers. It was cramped, but there were few arguments over offices: if we were running out of space, then it was a sure sign that we needed to sell a business.

It felt like a start-up, and was structured like one – I had taken a sizable pay cut from Reed Elsevier in exchange for a share of the business. The journals all had editors but in many ways the essence of the business was techie in nature with database programmers, software engineers and designers. The average age of the staff was younger than and also much more cosmopolitan. It was an office which would, to contemporary eyes, seem familiar. Gone were the suits and ties, the mandatory black leather shoes and editors with elbow patches. Gone too were the secretaries having letters dictated to them, the clacking of typewriters and huge piles of paper.

Everyone had a desktop computer at work and also a laptop at home, and we all used email to communicate. At Reed Elsevier, some of the executives' company cars did have phones, but mobile phones were still rare and frowned upon – Ian Irvine had been known to eject people from meetings if their phone rang. I had actually first been shown a mobile by an executive at Motorola during my course at Harvard, but it wasn't until I joined Current Science that I regularly used one. Smoking in the office was still very much allowed, but I had, at long last, managed to give up.

THE ART OF THE PUBLISHING DEAL

After a couple of years, we felt that we had taken *Current Biology* as far as we could. Vitek had always hoped that it would become a serious rival to *Nature* and while that hadn't happened, it had grown into a successful journal in its own right, with a strong editorial team. The offices were crammed, and it was time to sell.

It was at this point that Vitek came into his own. Vitek knew better than anyone I've ever met how to value, and how to sell, a publishing business. Despite the fact that most of the journal titles generally sold fewer than a few hundred copies, he insisted on a freshly designed colour cover for each issue. I did some analysis which showed that we could save £200k a year if we moved to generic covers, but when I took this to Vitek he slowly shook his head and (rightly) told me how little I understood. As he went on to explain, when it came to selling the business, the buyer would be looking to pay us roughly ten times our profits, and that this would be difficult to calculate as we didn't make any. But one of the things they would see is that we are wasting £200,000 a year on covers, and will duly factor this by a multiple of ten. And so it transpired.

In order to sell *Current Biology*, we needed to bundle it up and create a more substantial entity to attract a buyer. Although Vitek had a strong affection for BioMedNet, it was expensive to run and we knew that it would need to be sold along with *Current Biology* to make it more alluring to a publisher, with the promise of greater growth potential and a business model opaque enough for it to be difficult to accurately value. We already had Reed Elsevier in mind for it – Vitek had never sold a business to them before, but we knew that they wanted better engagement with the scientific community, and that BioMedNet would help to dispel the perception that all they did was sell high-cost subscriptions to established journals.

We approached Nigel Stapleton, who had been the chief financial officer of Reed International and was on the executive board of Reed Elsevier. We explained that it was important that BioMedNet should be managed on the Reed rather than the Elsevier side of the business as, whatever they might say, it would never flourish within Elsevier, and would just be seen as a competitor to their own journals. Nigel well understood this, but it wasn't long before twenty or so Elsevier executives began to get involved. This meant that there was an enormous process of negotiation and horse trading, with the inevitable wrangles about non-compete agreements. These were as pointless as ever – as Vitek always said, imposing a non-compete for 12 months is almost a cast-iron guarantee that the vendor will start to compete on the day it expires, having spent the year planning how to create a new business that is better than the one that's just been sold.

As part of the process, Reed Elsevier conducted a comprehensive due diligence exercise, and this included an examination of the leadership team's competencies and capabilities. A human resources executive from Amsterdam duly came over to spend two days in the Current Science office interviewing us all. She completed her analysis and then asked if she could use my email in order to send her report back to the head office. She did this, but (despite my telling her to do so) failed to delete her email. And so, once she had left, we read through their assessment of us. It was clear that, despite buying the business, Reed Elsevier didn't think much of its leadership team, and wanted shot of Vitek and me as soon as possible. Neither of us were surprised when, a couple of years later, they closed down BioMedNet.

It would be the last thing I did with Current Science. While Vitek was in Amsterdam going over the last details of the contract, Andrew Crompton was in the London office telling the staff what was going on, and I was in Frankfurt on the phone to both while at the same time negotiating to go and run Macmillan. I still owned 10% of Current Science Group, but it didn't feel right to continue having a share in Vitek's business if I wasn't working with him. So we agreed that I would take a share of the deal we had just done, and that would be it. What I didn't know was that Vitek would shortly go on to sell *Current Drugs* for tens of millions to Thomson Reuters. Although, by way of compensation, on the night he did this deal he took me out for a very nice dinner and we are still the best of friends.

MULTIMEDIA CD-ROMS

While Vitek and I were working together at Current Science, the British publishing industry as a whole was waking up to the new possibilities being wrought by digital technology. Of course, very few people knew what they were doing and a lot of money was wasted. At Reed International, we had set up an e-commerce site for Secker & Warburg, in the vague hope of selling our titles directly to consumers if, by some chance, anyone ever found us on the internet. It hadn't worked, but it had been an interesting experiment, cost relatively little, and the feeling at the time was very much that people had to try something, anything.

For many publishers in the 1990s, the internet seemed too frightening and chaotic for rights holders, while connections were still too slow and erratic for users, particularly outside the workplace. Most interest to begin with was instead offline, in CD-ROMs and the field of multimedia publishing. The home computer market in the mid-1990s was booming with a new generation of personal computers that had sound cards, 256-colour monitors and CD-ROM drives. While floppy discs had been able to store little more than a megabyte of information, the CD-ROM could take 650 Mb, a leap so huge that it promised to be all one would ever need.

Publishers such as Chadwyck-Healey which in the 1970s and 80s had been producing reference works on microfilm now quickly moved onto CD-ROMs, but it was a wider trend and almost everyone at some point tried multimedia – and lost money in the process. Science publishers looked to make multimedia versions of their textbooks, and there was particular interest in medicine, with Elsevier lavishly producing the *Sobotta Atlas of Human Anatomy* on CD-ROM. Faber released a CD ROM of T.S. Eliot's *The Wasteland*, with actors reciting the poem and filmed interviews with academic experts, while Thames & Hudson made elaborate multimedia art dictionaries. The CEO of Penguin waved a CD-ROM about astrophysics at Pearson's annual general meeting and proclaimed it was the future of publishing. For a while I joined the board of First Information Group, which produced interactive CD-ROMs of military history for the US market, on the basis that guns and weaponry always sell (except not enough to support the business). As with video games today, so publishers in the 1990s were not only hiring software developers but also commissioning film directors, animators, music composers and artists and the production costs could be enormous. The difference, of course, is that a blockbuster video game will sell in its millions, books in their thousands if you're lucky.

Although it seemed innovative and cutting edge at the time, publishers were essentially just trying to replicate books. As with the great project that had taken up such enormous manpower and resources in the 1980s, the second edition of the OED, the added functionality was still quite limited and not necessarily valued by consumers. It was much the same with the BBC's Domesday Project, an enormous geographical and social survey of the country which had been produced for LaserDisc. While being able to speedily search text was undoubtedly useful, many of the additions to multimedia were less so, and smacked of publishers wanting to come up with something new for the sake of it, rather than customers actually demanding them. Vitek always loved a new gadget and technology, but from our perspective at Current Science, there was nothing very interesting about the business model – these were still products, with a one-off sale to the consumer. Nor was there anything innovative about the distribution – they mainly ended up stacked awkwardly on the shelves of bookshops, having cost a great deal to produce, and where they largely failed to sell.

Publishers could make money from making multimedia titles, but only by persuading someone else to pay for them. As is often the case, it was the pharmaceuticals companies who stumped up for many of these. A number of lavish medical and physiology CD-ROMs were produced with animations, music and video footage, and cheerfully sent out to doctors and health care providers, many of them never to be taken out of their boxes.

The only really successful mass market CD-ROMs were the ones that were bundled up with the purchase of computers – just as Dick Brass had intended for his first spell checkers. Britannica's CD-ROM encyclopedia, launched in 1995 and priced at upwards of $1000, was a costly flop and not long afterwards the entire business, which dated back to the 18th century, was sold at a knockdown price and never recovered. By contrast, Microsoft's multimedia encyclopedia *Encarta* started out retailing for $400 but the price was quickly lowered before being integrated into bundling deals with PC retailers. Millions of copies were distributed across Europe and the US as sales of computers to homes and schools boomed, until the arrival of Wikipedia immediately rendered it obsolete.

Of course, one of the things that almost all of us missed was that, in the digital age, people would crave something far more traditional than interactive multimedia – the audio book. Very few foresaw that audio books would be such a big thing, and that in 2022 almost all of them would be unabridged. In the 1990s, Reed and all the other publishers had sold audio versions of their leading books on tape and later on CD.

In the usually under-resourced and neglected audio books departments, one of the principal tasks would be to produce abridged versions of texts, because otherwise they would require far too many tapes – a problem that disappeared with the advent of broadband internet.

INNOVATION AND ADDING VALUE

Money was being lost on CD-ROMs, but there were plenty of publishers in the late 1990s who were starting to see how digital technologies could be used to create new kinds of publishing business and add real value. One of these was Adam Hodgkin, who had been a philosophy editor at OUP, but had taken an interest in electronic publishing from an early stage and co-founded Xrefer along with Daryl Rayner, who had previously been at Current Science, and two others. The company struck deals with reference book publishers to digitise their texts to provide access across a large number of reference works. The aim was to have libraries, schools and universities subscribe on behalf of their users. With dictionaries (general and subject-based), encyclopaedias and other texts collected together, along with search functionality and hyperlinking, it quickly became a much-used resource.

That didn't mean that growing the business was straightforward. In 2000 I joined the board, which also involved investing a bit to get over some of the inevitable humps in the road prior to finding a long-term investor. There was then the familiar problem that the founding directors failed to see eye to eye with the new investors, and, as so often happens, a new management team was put in place with the attendant disruption. But the business continued to grow steadily, particularly in the US, and Xrefer became Credo Reference, which sounded more authoritative but also, I suspect, made things easier in the internet era, in which the letter X has become synonymous with pornography. Some years later it was acquired by the American publisher Infobase, so all the original founders and investors made money, and its headquarters are now in Boston.

Around the same time, half a dozen of the largest scientific publishers came together to establish Crossref. It was an all-too-rare instance of an industry collaboration that has actually proved to be successful. Crossref is a not-for-profit organisation that enables the electronic linking of academic references from one journal to another, irrespective of the publisher. Crucially, it not only provides the technical connectivity but also manages the micropayments between different publishers, so that the researcher can seamlessly move from one article to another. There are now more than 17,000 members around the world, responsible for publishing more than a hundred million articles. As any former student over the age of 40 will know, up until then if you wanted to follow up a refence in a journal, you would have to go through the laborious process of making a note of it, and then digging out the relevant publication which, if you were lucky, would also be held in the same library.

Current Science, Xrefer and Crossref were very different kinds of entity (a privately owned publisher, an investment-driven start-up, an industry body), but they were all examples of how at the end of the century, publishing was starting to use digital technologies to create things that were genuinely new and useful – in a way that CD-ROMS often didn't. What these and other companies were trying to do wasn't so different from Dick Brass and his floppy disc dictionaries in the late 1970s – by focusing on the needs of readers, users and researchers, it would be possible for publishers to deliver value and build successful businesses in the internet age.

THE RISE AND RISE OF JOURNAL PUBLISHING

At Current Science, we had never shown much interest in book publishing. For Vitek, it was the innovations that were taking place in scientific content, software and communications and that meant his focus was on journals. By way of contrast, there had been no journal publishing at all at Harrap, although while I was there one enterprising editor had started to develop a loose leaf service for human resource professionals. This had actually been quite profitable, but no one within senior management was much interested and it eventually petered out.

Pergamon had been very different, with Maxwell all too aware of the sizable market and growth potential for journal publishing. But when I had started at OUP in 1975 it probably had no more than twenty journal titles in total – far fewer than Cambridge University Press at the time. It was an eclectic list that included *Notes and Queries*, the long-running

Victorian journal dedicated to the history of the English language, *Early Music* and some linguistics journals. There were only a handful of science journals, which partly reflected OUP's bias towards the humanities, but also the feeling that journal articles were things that academics wrote before writing the standard monograph or textbook. Journal editors were appointed in the hope that they would become leading book authors. While Pergamon and Blackwell Scientific were busy meeting with scientists and learned societies, developing journal ideas, launching new titles and building up subscribers, OUP was still wedded to the primacy of the book. There was no appreciation that a strong journal would help to frame and shape a field of academic study, and therefore become an enduring source of interest and income.

This low status was reflected in the fact that journal production was located in Neasden, as part of the warehouse distribution facility rather than within publishing in London or Oxford. Journals didn't start to be taken seriously and move into the core of the business until OUP acquired *Brain*, the neurology journal. This happened largely by accident. It had been offloaded by Macmillan and the neurologist, Ian Macdonald, who previously oversaw it was a fellow Kiwi and friend of Dan Davin, who was happy to do the deal. It was the first time OUP began to see that science journals could be highly lucrative – we kept 25% of all revenue, and also made good margins on the production which was undertaken by OUP's printing division.

Over the course of the 1980s, as academic research continued to grow around the world, it became ever clearer how valuable journal publishing had become. After the success of *Brain*, OUP had at last begun to take notice. The reorganisation of the company and the closing down of the Neasden site was helpful in this regard, as it meant that journal publishing became located in the main headquarters in Oxford, and a dedicated journals publisher was appointed.

Over the next few years, OUP acquired and launched titles, and developed some particular strengths in mathematics and chemistry. We were fortunate to buy up Information Retrieval Ltd. This was a small family-run journal publisher, whose owner had died suddenly while on holiday and, through John Manger, a highly professional science publisher, we were able to acquire it without going to auction for around £2m. Within this business were two highly successful journals, *European Molecular Biology Organisation* and *Nucleic Acid Research*. But the family's finances and business affairs had become so intertwined that the company recorded almost no profits at all – even the cost of repatriating the owner's body and his funeral had come out of the company. The result was that the balance sheet was so meagre that we able to buy the company for far less than the journals were actually worth. As part of this deal, we also took on Martin Richardson, an excellent publisher who became a key figure in growing OUP's journals division.

Today OUP publishes more than five hundred journals. But it was Robert Maxwell who had benefited from the crucial first mover advantage, launching many of the leading journals in a range of fields, and in 1991 he was able to sell Pergamon to Elsevier for £440 million. This was regarded by many at the time as a hefty price for what was considered to be a mature business, but Elsevier industrialised Maxwell's ingenuity and entrepreneurial chaos, bringing their protestant corporate sensibility to bear. Over the following decade, Elsevier consolidated and steadily grew what he had created, building up a vast range of journal titles that could be harvested for substantial revenues year in year out. They also had the Heinemann-Butterworth titles from Reed, and would always be ready to buy out Vitek and anyone else who was coming up with new journals or innovations that could pose a threat to their supremacy.

It is worth noting that, while highly profitable when established, journals are difficult and resource intensive to set up. Market intelligence and careful research and consultation are needed to find the right niche. A new journal needs a good, ambitious editor with excellent contacts to put together a strong board made up of leading academics – and this usually entails plenty of expensive dinners. Marketing a new journal is tough, and you need sales people to go and persuade librarians to take out subscriptions. But once you've done all this and if you've been able to get a journal established, then the publisher is in a very good position. They become regarded as essential for keeping up with the field, subscriptions keep coming in, the ongoing editorial and production costs are relatively low, and it generates excellent and sustainable profits.

Maxwell had understood all this and, just as he had also foreseen all those years ago, it would be the life sciences that would be central to journal publishing – a vast subject area, with a multitude of specific issues, research topics and questions, each of which warranted its own journal. By the 2000s Reed Elsevier's scientific publishing operations would be generating annual profits in excess of half a billion pounds. But it was the margins on the journals, coming in at over 30%, which were really striking, and which meant that governments and funding bodies would start to take notice.

CHAPTER SEVEN: A GLOBAL FAMILY BUSINESS

How Macmillan became a global player; the evolution of Nature; journal publishing comes up against the Open Access movement; Google, the biggest threat of them all; outsourcing in India; children's publishing grows up; accidental successes and negotiating with an imprisoned author; the diversions and distractions of management; from industry blagger to blogger.

This story of a Victorian family business transformed and subsumed by international corporations in the era of global capitalism is a familiar one, and something that the publishing industry knows all too well. Through successive iterations of mergers, deals and take-overs, the ownership structure of British publishing has radically changed in the last fifty years. It had happened to Harrap, the first company I had worked for, to Pergamon, to Reed International Books and, in the late 1990s, a similar fate awaited Macmillan.

The company had been founded in London in the 1843 by two brothers, Daniel and Alexander Macmillan, from the Isle of Arran off the west coast of Scotland. Daniel had been running a bookshop and had the commercial instincts which, when combined with Alexander's editorial flair, formed the basis for one of Britain's most enduring publishing houses. Many of the greatest names from the golden age of 19th century English literature were published by Macmillan: Lewis Carroll, Matthew Arnold, Charles Kingsley, Alfred Tennyson, Thomas Hardy and Rudyard Kipling. In the same period, the company founded *Nature* magazine and the *Grove Dictionary of Music and Musicians*. This was sustained over the next century, with Macmillan at the heart of the British literary and cultural establishment – Daniel's grandson, Harold Macmillan, worked at the company for twenty years while rising up the ranks of the Conservative Party to become Prime Minister. After retiring from frontline politics, he returned as Lord Stockton to chair Macmillan until his death in the 1986, and the company continued to be led by his grandsons, Alex and David.

But by the late 1990s, the company had run out of stream and the family had lost interest in taking it further, with Alex (now Lord Stockton) more intent on pursuing a political career. And so, after 150 years and five generations, the majority of Macmillan was sold for approximately £400 million to Dieter von Holtzbrinck who along with his sister Monica owned the Holtzbrinck Publishing Group. While not as venerable as Macmillan, the company still had an impressive pedigree. It had been founded by their father Georg before the war as a book club, and by the time his heirs inherited it in the 1980s, it had grown into an extensive media and publishing group, with notable assets including the *Die Zeit* newspaper, Handelsblatt, Scientific American, Henry Holt, Farrar Straus and the distinguished Fischer, Rowohlt, and Droemer publishing houses. Monica was content to run Fischer, while Dieter took control of the rest of the business.

Acquiring a controlling stake in Macmillan represented a significant gamble. Dieter had wanted to make Holtzbrinck a genuinely global business, and to match the success of their great German competitor, Bertelsmann. The outgoing chief executive of Macmillan, Nicky Byam Shaw, was charged with finding a successor and put me on the shortlist. After a meeting with Dieter in Stuttgart, it was agreed that I would head up the UK and worldwide business, with the US operation (St. Martin's Press and related interests) being run as a separate business. Dieter was frank with me – he had taken a big risk, he was under pressure and would need help to make it work.

All publishing companies are to a certain extent a curate's egg, and this was certainly true of Macmillan when I started there. The reach of its activities was extensive and thoroughly international. As well as Macmillan on the trade side, with the Pan and Picador paperback imprints, there was Peninsula Publishing Company (a printing brokerage in China) and Macmillan India, a sprawling typesetting operation with offices in Delhi, Jaipur, Bangalore and Kochi. And amidst all of this, there was Macmillan Magazines, which was based in King's Cross and the publisher of three major titles – *Nursing Times, Health Services Journal* and something called *Nature*.

NURTURING NATURE

Under German corporate law, there is a two-tier governance structure: the management board composed of executive directors and the supervisory board (Beirat), which among other things has the power to appoint and dismiss members of the former. Shortly after I started at Macmillan, Dieter invited me to Stuttgart to meet the supervisory board (or supermisery board as we liked to call it). At this meeting, a member of the board asked whether £400m for Macmillan really represented a good investment. Dieter tried to allay their fears by excitedly telling them that it had been a wonderful decision, because now they owned the highly prestigious Picador imprint. I could see that they were going to need something more concrete than that, and so declared to them: "You've got *Nature*. I think it's worth £250m now and I think it could be worth £500m." I was greeted with a sceptical silence.

Notwithstanding my efforts to impress the board, I really did believe it. *Nature* was of course already at this point a publishing legend. Along with *The Lancet* and *Science*, it is one of the very few scientific journals with at least some levels of awareness among the general public. Dating back to the 1860s when it was founded by Alexander Macmillan with the astronomer Norman Lockyer, it had started life as an 'a weekly illustrated journal of science', a forum for 'men of science' as Lockyer called them, to write about their work and bring their discoveries to the general population. Its very first article was written by Thomas Henry Huxley and for much of its early history it was associated with similarly progressively-minded scientists, becoming in particular a focal point for the controversies around Darwin's theory of evolution that so wracked Victorian society. But, despite Macmillan and Lockyer's original vision, *Nature* would become a journal less for the public and more for the burgeoning scientific community. This would continue and throughout its existence, *Nature* has been the means by which many of the greatest scientific breakthroughs have been announced to the world: the discovery of the neutron, nuclear fission, the structure of DNA, plate tectonics and the hole in the ozone layer, were all first covered in *Nature* papers. For all of this time, it had been owned by Macmillan and grown steadily in international prominence – by the time that Holtzbrinck had bought the company, it had more than 200 staff and offices in New York, Washington, Paris and Tokyo alongside its headquarters in London.

Despite all this, there was still huge growth potential. Vitek had long been fascinated by *Nature*, and when he came to see me not long after I started, he observed: "It's not really a journal you've got, it's a whole business." He was right, and turning it into a publishing company would become my priority. This became easier once we had sold *Nursing Times*. Founded as a weekly magazine in 1905 it was, at least outside of the US, the world's largest periodical for the nursing profession. It was making Macmillan a decent profit but there were concerns about its long-term over-reliance on classified advertising. So, in 1998 we ran an auction which EMAP won. The sale freed up office space in King's Cross, gave us some capital and allowed us to concentrate on growing *Nature*.

One of the first things we did was to stop calling the company Macmillan Magazines and changed it to Nature Publishing Group. In Basingstoke, the relatively under-cherished Stockton Press was rebranded as Nature Publishing as well. We were creating a scientific publishing house out of its original single journal base and so set about launching a dozen new journals a year, with titles such as *Nature Climate Change*, *Nature Neuroscience*, *Nature Immunology*. Each was put together with a first-class editor and would cost at least a million pounds to launch, and nearly every one became the number one journal by impact factor. Today there are more than sixty such titles (including review journals), ranging from *Nature Aging* to *Nature Urology*.

The first managing director of Nature Publishing Group came to us in unusual circumstances. Dieter and his sister had a much younger half-brother, Stefan, who had recently joined the business. Being so much younger, Dieter saw him as representing the next generation of the family and wanted him to lead the business into the future. So it was agreed that he could learn in London by becoming managing director of Nature Publishing Group under my guidance. This was hardly how executive recruitment would normally be done, but it was still a family-owned business and Stefan proved to be an energetic and imaginative director, committed to maintaining the highest editorial standards and willing to embrace change.

The company grew quickly, and we hired many more people. The days when a hapless young man could become a medical editor at OUP on the basis of little more than having a science degree and mentioning the term catecholamines were long gone. Most of the editors we hired at Nature Publishing had doctorates and a background in scientific research.

They had in-depth knowledge of the field and the people in it. We were able to develop partnerships, and generate papers, with the top scientific institutes and projects of the time. The biggest of these at the turn of the millennium was the Human Genome project. There were two parties racing to sequence the entire genome – an international consortium of universities led by the National Institutes of Health in the US and Celera, a private corporation that was hoping to commercially exploit some of the data. Nature partnered with the NIH to publish a series of special issues and ensure that the methods, sequence data and initial analysis were widely available from an early stage.

The Nature Publishing Group brand was being created and when Stefan returned to Stuttgart as chief executive of the whole Holtzbrinck Group we appointed Annette Thomas, editor of Nature Reviews, as his successor. A neuroscientist by training, she moved from having a relatively junior editorial role to being managing director, but we had no doubt that Annette would be able to do the job, and she immediately instigated some vital changes.

Up until then, half of NPG revenue had come from advertising, of which roughly half again had been classified job ads and the other half display. We took a calculated risk by offering the small ads free in the hope that this would increase traffic substantially and make NPG an even more central part of the scientific community. In the mid-1990s, *Nature* had a circulation of 60,000 and so an estimated readership of about 200,000 individuals, but within a few years the readership was in the millions. This in turn substantially increased the amount we could charge for display adverts. It was the kind of strategy that has become familiar with internet brands and digital media platforms – an aggressive drive to grow the audience or membership, and to generate income further down the line.

And there were many avenues for doing this. Digitizing all of our back issues was a big undertaking, but it kept the scientific record alive, and became part of a new, higher priced subscription service that proved to be extremely popular – as the history of science has grown as a subject, so historians as well as scientists wanted to study classic *Nature* papers. And the cost and trouble of tracking down missing journal titles for those libraries that wanted a complete collection became a thing of the past.

Entirely new roles in publishing were coming into being: interactive designers, web analytics, content management system builders and database programmers. Marketing and sales roles had also become much more technical. Previously, journal publishers had blithely sold print copies to university libraries and no one really knew how often, or if at all, they were being read. Now there was a plethora of measurement tools which meant that librarians, and also publishers, could track usage. Marketing teams had to demonstrate that journal articles in *Nature*, and everywhere else, were actually being read, and a whole new science of metrics and quantifying impact came into being. Where once circulation and citations were the benchmarks, anyone working in journal publishing today needs to have mastery of downloads, video plays, blog comments, page impressions, click throughs, social media mentions and much else besides.

Along with the appointment of Annette Thomas to this key role British publishing was making progress in other spheres – Gail Rebuck had become chief executive of Random House in the early 1990s, Victoria Barnsley would become head of HarperCollins UK, and any number of strong female publishing executives were making their mark in the US and UK – although perhaps less rapidly in the non-English-speaking worlds. Under Annette's leadership, the company went from strength to strength. By 2007, NPG had revenues in the region of £140m and £40m profit, and employed five hundred people in offices around the world. When Nature Publishing, Macmillan Education and Springer Science merged in 2015 to form Springer Nature, the Macmillan elements (largely Nature Publishing Group) were valued at approximately 2bn Euros. The 'illustrated journal' that Alexander Macmillan had founded so that Victorian society could keep abreast of the latest scientific discoveries had come a long way. But while Nature was thriving, journal publishing in general was facing up to a new challenge.

OPEN ACCESS TAKES ON JOURNAL PUBLISHING

"What would be the effect on your business and the industry if your requirements to obtain copyright were outlawed as an onerous term and there were restrictions placed on inducements to assigning copyright?"

It was the spring of 2004, and I was in front of the House of Commons Select Committee on Science and Technology. This question, one of many, had just been posed by Paul Farrelly, MP. Alongside me were some of my greatest competitors and oldest friends: Bob Campbell, President of Blackwell and John Jarvis from Wiley. On this afternoon, we were putting aside our commercial rivalry and trying to make the case for a business model that had endured for centuries, a concept so fundamental to publishing that, just a few years previously, we could never have considered it ever being questioned. But here we were – trying to justify the principle that people should pay for published content, rather than being able to access it for free.

The Open Access movement had begun with a group of ideologically-driven scientists, who felt that science was being held back by publishers and that the results of all research should be made available online, free of charge. Digitalisation and the reduction in production, printing and distribution costs, meant that some felt that the traditional role of the publisher was becoming obsolete. This was by no means a representative group – most researchers didn't really mind, provided they were able to get published and the journal was doing a good job of maintaining editorial quality and reach among the scientific community. But the group was a noisy, well-connected and articulate one, and criticism was amplified by the profits that certain academic publishers were making. The main culprit in this regard was Elsevier, whose margins were considered by many to be obscene – although certainly not by their shareholders! While Nature Publishing Group employed a large number of in-house editorial staff, Elsevier outsourced most editorial decision-making to its external academic journal editors in universities and research institutes and these tended to be largely unpaid or subsidised by their institution. What's more, as a publicly-listed company, unlike Macmillan and Blackwell, Reed Elsevier was obliged to publish how profitable it was in order to maintain its share price and reward its shareholders through dividends.

Some of the major research funders, particularly the Wellcome Trust, shared these concerns and exacerbated long-held complaints that far too much of the credit for scientific research had being going to publishers rather than themselves. It's worth saying that Vitek was also an early champion for open access – not least, because he was already thinking of how he could come up with new companies based on the business model. A number of journalists were covering the issue and championed the Open Access cause – as professionals who wrote for a living, they often struggled to understand why academic authors were not similarly paid for their articles. With prominent scientists, commentators and funders all raising the matter, it was inevitable that the politicians would start to take an interest, and so the House of Commons Select Committee decided to haul us in.

As the three of us tried to explain to the MPs that afternoon, there was a misunderstanding of what journal publishers actually did, and what people were paying for. Alongside production, design, technology and much else, the principal cost of publishing scientific articles in *Nature* or anywhere else was the editorial expertise, and in particular managing the peer review process. It was this, above all else, that researchers regarded as fundamental and which had to be paid for. It can be funded through university library budgets or else by the authors themselves or their funders (and given the interests of commercial sponsors and pharmaceutical companies, this could be far more problematic). Simplistically, in the former case you could have a thousand major university libraries in the world paying, say, $1 million a year to generate $1billion to cover costs, or a million authors each paying $1000. From a purely economic lens the former must be more efficient.

We probably didn't help our cause when one of us told the Committee that making medical research freely available to everyone was a bad idea and that "This rather enticing statement that everybody should be able to see everything could lead to chaos. Speak to people in the medical profession, and they will say the last thing they want is people who may have illnesses reading this information and asking things."

He may have been right, but it was exactly this perception of exclusivity, and that publishers knew best, that was helping to fuel the Open Access movement. There was a feeling that academic editors were not making scientific information available, but rather suppressing and controlling it, and for all the arguments we made that afternoon in Parliament, we all knew that it was not going to go away. Over the following years Open Access was to bring about some significant changes and is still evolving. One thing for sure is that the old comfortable and efficient model was disappearing fast.

This is not just the case for commercial publishers. Something not always appreciated by the advocates for Open Access is that one of the great beneficiaries of the traditional model of journal publishing had been the learned societies. These not-for-profit organisations, of which there are more than a hundred in the UK, exist to promote an academic discipline or profession and have often played a crucial role in the development of science and research around the world. Almost all learned societies either have in-house publishing divisions or else contractual agreements with academic publishers, and these can be substantial operations. The Royal Society has a dozen journals, including *Philosophical Transactions*, which dates back to 1665 and can lay claim to being the world's first English language scientific periodical. The reason that the Royal Society, the Institute of Physics and similar learned societies have been able to do so much excellent work promoting science in schools, offering scholarships, helping students from disadvantaged backgrounds and hosting public events is in large part because of their earnings from journal publishing.

This is no longer the case in the same way. Twenty years since Open Access first emerged, the landscape of academic publishing is a much more fragmented and complicated place – for publishers, learned societies, libraries and also authors. Publishing has become arguably more universal, but also less efficient. Many publishers now have hybrid journals, which are part pure open access, and part traditional subscriptions, depending on who is paying. Negotiations and licensing agreements have become extraordinarily complex leading to much higher administrative costs. Learned societies can no longer rely on journal subscription earnings, but any hopes in some quarters that Open Access would reduce the profitability of publishers seem to have been misplaced so far – Elsevier's parent company, the unpronounceable RELX, declared more than £2bn in profit in 2021, and their margins are as healthy as ever.

One significant change, which rarely came up in the industry debates, is that Open Access has meant that advertising and marketing has had to be transformed. In the traditional model, the publisher naturally wanted to promote its journals, so that academics and researchers were aware of their value, and requested that university librarians would subscribe to them. In the new world of Open Access, however, the markets to be addressed are the funding agencies and the authors themselves. Everything is geared to satisfying them.

Whether the general public has benefited it's hard to say. The point may have been made too bluntly in front of the MPs but it wasn't necessarily incorrect: scientific journals are produced by and for scientists, and the crucial issue is not how easily they can be read by the general public, but rather how well they provide up-to-date, accurate and high-quality content for the professionals that need it.

DO NO EVIL: GOING TO BATTLE
AGAINST A TECH GIANT

It wasn't just politicians and government regulators that we had to worry about. As the digital economy grew, and the internet expanded into more walks of life, so a new generation of companies started to impact on publishing. In 1999, Amazon launched in the UK but few publishers I knew saw this as an immediate threat. On the contrary, it was a new way of selling books. At Reed and Macmillan we had experimented with selling titles directly to the public online through our own branded websites without much success. Amazon offered a way to do this without the enormous investment in technology, marketing and distribution, and they were not, at least to begin with, demanding unreasonable discounts from publishers.

Ultimately Amazon wanted what we wanted – to sell books. But Google was a different story altogether. It was almost exactly halfway through my 50-year story, in 1998, that the company was founded. It is arguably the single company that has brought the biggest change, and threat, to the publishing industry, but it took some years before publishers woke up to this.

It was in 2004 that Google launched its Library Project, in which the company announced it was going to make available online free of charge all of the information held in the world's libraries. This had been a dream of Google's founders when they had still been graduate students, and there had long been schemes with similar visions. Project Gutenberg, the oldest digital library, had been founded back in 1971 when a student had retyped the United States Declaration of Independence and then transmitted it over the university computer network. Over the next three decades volunteers had painstakingly typed and scanned hundreds of out-of-copyright classics of western literature and made them freely available on CD-ROMs or else hosted on university servers. But by the early 2000s Google wanted to take this to an entirely new level.

No one in the publishing world had any objection to Google digitizing works that were out of copyright, and the scanning of historical documents from libraries was only to be welcomed. But Google were unable to stop themselves, and it soon became apparent that their intention was actually to digitise and make available every book they could get their hands on – irrespective of the author, publisher or its copyright status.

Publishers were told that if they didn't want their books to be subjected to this process, then they needed to inform Google beforehand. This would have entailed a considerable administrative burden, and turned upside down a fundamental concept of copyright: the principle that all literary (and artistic and musical) works are automatically given protection at the moment of creation without the need for documentation.

Publishers around the world were aghast. Google was denounced by publishing trade bodies and some companies were so appalled that all of their staff were instructed not to use the Google search engine – although it is highly doubtful if Google themselves actually noticed this. In the US, the Association of American Publishers and the Authors' Guild took the lead and supported a legal challenge to Google by their members.

I had my own skirmish in the war against Google when I perpetrated the 'Google heist'. I was with Ruediger Salat, head of trade books at Holtzbrinck in Germany, at Book Expo America in 2007, when we happened to walk past Google's exhibition stand. It was suitably enormous: hosted by dozens of publicity officers, with industry figures enjoying the drinks and canapes. There was a bank of laptop computers below the Google banner and their famous (now retracted) motto, "Do No Evil". However, there was no signage specifying that these laptops belonged to them, and so we decided to 'borrow' one and took it to a nearby table along with our drinks. It wasn't long before a nonplussed Google staffer approached and asked why we had removed one of their laptops. She was even more bemused when I pleasantly told her: "You can have it back if you like."

She said – yes please, and I told her that: "Nowhere on the stand was it specified that you didn't want us to take it. It's just like Google Library."

At this point, she was joined by colleagues, security had been alerted and not long afterwards the laptop was returned. The kerfuffle at Book Expo America would have gone unnoticed if I hadn't then drawn attention to it with what was my most-ever read blogpost. Wantonly incriminating myself with photographic evidence, I described our 'heist' and it soon went viral - although I didn't know that as

Book Expo America June 2007

a social media term. It was picked up by mainstream media, and there were plenty of publishers and commentators willing to wade in.

The Google heist made news for no more than a couple of days, but it was part of a longer guerrilla war between publishers and Google that went on for some years, a war that ultimately Google didn't so much lose as lost interest in. The ongoing rows, negative publicity and legal battles with publishers wore them down, and ultimately the financial benefits to Google from the undertaking were trivial compared to their advertising revenues: by 2020, the company was earning in excess of $200bn a year, a far higher turnover than the entire global publishing industry. Google has done, and continues to do, excellent work digitizing rare and ancient manuscripts from the great libraries and collections of the world but, at the moment at least, no longer feels the need to undermine copyright.

MACMILLAN INDIA: AN IMPERIAL LEGACY

Outside of Europe, the country that I spent most time in while at Macmillan was India, a country which was driving change and bringing huge efficiencies to publishing at the turn of the 21st century.

This was by no means unexpected. As long ago as 1979 one of my suggestions at OUP had been that we might move typesetting from Oxford to India. This did eventually happen, but it took a long time to get there – and by then Macmillan and many others had been doing it for years. India has sometimes been considered a difficult place to do publishing, with various logistical and commercial shortcomings, but it has always had some fundamental assets. The country has a legal system which, whilst complex, is based on British law and so understood by most of the world, while they have a democratic constitution that guarantees freedom of expression, which is essential for successful publishing.

In the nineteenth century, India was seen as a natural extension for British business and Macmillan had been one of the first publishers to ship books (mainly educational) to India and to have offices there. The story goes that the company dispatched two general managers, one for the east based in Calcutta, one for the west in Bombay. They each served the firm loyally for several decades but the distances and difficulties of travelling between the two cities were such that they only met in person on the ship taking them back to Britain for their retirement.

From these colonial beginnings, a large publishing enterprise had grown up. There were Macmillan offices in every major city, with separate offices and structures for general books, academic and science. In 1970 a typesetting division was launched in Bangalore, primarily to provide services across the company. By the late 1990s this was employing almost 2000 people and undertaking a vast amount of work, not just for Macmillan but also for other major STM companies such as Wiley and Elsevier. Given the nature of its services for scientific journals, it needed skilled and technically able workers and we generally employed graduates with a good knowledge of English.

When I visited one of the offices in Delhi, I had my first experience of a high-tech business in a developing country as I waded through narrow streets blocked by cows to find a run-down building, with the most enormous satellite dish I had ever seen perched precariously from its summit. The apparent disorder and congestion of Indian cities belied a workforce that was highly professional. In the late 1970s when I had visited OUP's office in Delhi, I had been struck by the huge number of typists, and been told that because of the absence of photocopiers and the high cost of making carbon copies, it was cheaper to employ people to type out copies of letters and other documents. But now, with digital technology, the Indian workforce was in a position to be truly productive. Most of the work was done in Bangalore with a large proportion of the staff coming out of the high-quality education system in Kerala.

The definition of typesetting was an expansive one. Copy editing, typesetting, proof checking were all key requirements. But as the skills and capacity grew, so did the range of services. This was crucial to the future of the company – Macmillan India's biggest client was Elsevier, but given how relentlessly they squeezed our costs, we needed to diversify and to grow our client base. Macmillan India was possibly the most entrepreneurial part of the whole Macmillan group, and the big success was when we landed the contract to publish Yellow Pages in North America. Suddenly, the company had to produce thousands of adverts for plumbers, electricians, Indian restaurants and everything else, and in an incredibly short space of time it trained up and deployed an army of designers who could produce advertisements appealing to US consumers.

CHILDREN'S PUBLISHING GROWS UP

One of the biggest growth areas in my time at Macmillan was children's publishing. In international terms, the UK is arguably as famous for children's literature as it is for Shakespeare and The Beatles. Over the course of the 60s and 70s, the legendary editor Kaye Webb had turned Puffin Books into the undisputed leader of children's publishing, releasing paperback versions of children's classics and establishing the Puffin Club with the vow to "make children into book readers". But it still took a surprisingly long time for mainstream publishers to fully appreciate this. At OUP, children's publishing had been barely considered at all by senior management – even though it had been home to some brilliant editors, authors and illustrators.

At Reed, through Heinemann and Methuen, we published famous children's book series such as Thomas the Tank Engine, Winnie the Pooh and Tintin. These are all much-loved characters, essential elements of our literary culture and huge international brands, but again were only belatedly given the level of focus and seriousness that they merited. The Winnie the Pooh books for instance, have sold more than fifty million copies worldwide and been translated into more than seventy languages. They are especially popular in Eastern Europe, with a street in Warsaw named after Pooh. No wonder that in 2001 the Disney corporation eventually paid $350million to buy up all of the rights – even though they expired in 2022, meaning that many of the characters and stories are now in the public domain.

At Reed, we had possession of the only oil painting of Pooh by E.H. Shepard whose line drawings did so much to enhance A.A. Milne's text. It has to be said that Shepard was nothing like as good in oil as he was with a pen, and he only did a single painting of Pooh, which was believed to be intended for a 1930s Bristol tearoom. Nevertheless, given Pooh's iconic status, this was a national art treasure and I was worried that it might get lost in the chaos as Reed Elsevier disposed of its literary assets. We tried to persuade the National Portrait Gallery to house it, but they declined on the dispiriting grounds that they only displayed portraits of people, not fictitious animals. Eventually the portrait was sold at auction, although at least it is on public display in the city of Winnipeg, the city that inspired the name of the black bear in London Zoo, who inspired Milne to give Pooh his Christian name.

Over the course of its history Macmillan had published some notable children's literature, dating all the way back to *Alice in Wonderland* and Charles Kingsley's *The Water Babies*. Into the 20th century, it had published Kipling's *Just so Stories*, not to mention countless volumes of Biggles. But it wasn't until the 1990s that the company really gave children's books the attention they deserved. This transformation was largely down to Kate Wilson who had started her career in publishing in the 1980s as a rights manager at Faber, and then moved across to build up children's publishing at Macmillan.

Kate brought a distinctive focus to the business, combining editorial flair with a strong focus on the bottom line. Her breakthrough title was *The Gruffalo*, by Julia Donaldson and Axel Schaeffler, which became an instant classic on its release in the late 1990s and over the last twenty years has sold something like 15 million copies. In the 2010s decade, Donaldson remained the UK's bestselling author, outselling the likes of J.K. Rowling and Jamie Oliver. It has spawned many different editions including jigsaw, pop-up, sticker, colouring-in and felt flap versions. Back in the early 1970s, when times had been hard at Harrap, we would try and do much the same with the Milly-Molly-Mandy book series, just as today editors and marketeers at Bloomsbury are ingeniously coming up with new formats for Harry Potter. The emotional relationship that a young reader has with a much-loved book doesn't just last a lifetime, but will be passed down the generations. More than this, and to the great advantage of the publisher, it also means there is often an affection for the physical book to a level that rarely exists in other kinds of publishing. Children's publishing is still largely print-based and looks set to continue that way, as parents and children still cherish the tactile sensation from holding and reading a book.

Kate went on to set up Nosy Crow with husband Adrian Soar as her Commercial Director. They have become hugely successful. Although it wasn't the first of its kind, a dedicated children's publisher was still distinctive – and certainly when I started in the industry, children's books were by and large regarded as merely a junior version of adult publishing. Now every publisher has an autonomous children's book division with expert dedicated editorial, marketing, design, and sales support but, as in academic publishing, it is frequently the small independents where true creativity flourishes.

ACCIDENTAL SUCCESSES

Back in Stuttgart, the 'supermisery board' were always calling for greater strategic focus. They would query why we had publishing interests in Zimbabwe or three offices in Namibia or so many different education companies. It was true that there were all manner of businesses, joint ventures, agreements and brands, many of which existed for historical reasons, but lack of focus didn't necessarily mean we couldn't make money. And actually, the strength of a large publishing company can be in its diversity. There is an old adage in Hollywood, coined by the screenwriter William Goldman, that 'nobody knows anything' – no matter how smart or experienced, nobody in the film industry knows what works and whether a film will be successful. And in many ways this is true of publishing as well – from talking rabbits to schoolboy wizards, the greatest sellers of the last half-century have never been predictable. But at least if you are large and diverse enough, then unexpected opportunities and accidental successes will arise – and the trick is to grab them when they do.

For instance, Macmillan had long been the publishers of Telegraph Books, which mainly consisted of crosswords and anthologies from the Telegraph newspapers. At some point in 2005, the Telegraph started running its first Sudoku puzzles, which we agreed to publish in book form and to handle the worldwide rights. It was soon apparent that we had unwittingly stumbled onto a global craze. Our little books, containing 150 pages of puzzles and another 50 pages of answers (which were actually needless, but meant we could justify producing 200-page books), conquered the world. We alerted the editor of *Die Zeit* a Holtzbrinck-owned weekly newspaper in Germany, who was sceptical, but was persuaded to run the puzzles. We also offered the licence to Holtzbrinck USA who declined, allowing us to sell North American rights to Peter Mayer at Overlook. Holtzbrinck USA, soon realizing their mistake, made amends by cleverly acquiring the rights to the New York Times Sudokus, thus ensuring that the Group as a whole had two mega bestsellers that year. One of the stranger aspects of these deals was that we were able to sell the translation rights – the beauty of Sudokus, of course, being that there were no actual words to translate.

We were to have even better luck with our distribution company in Swansea. In the mid-1990s, we had published a new edition of the

Grove's Dictionary of Music and Musicians, which by this point was more than twenty volumes in size and sold, as a complete set, for many hundreds of pounds. In order to avoid the discount granted to retailers, a dedicated company, Globe Publishing Services, was established to sell direct to libraries and wealthy music-loving customers. It was decided that it would be better if this operation was camouflaged to avoid a book-trade row, and so was based in a new facility in Swansea rather than Basingstoke (booksellers would have immediately connected Basingstoke parcels with Macmillan). Within a year or two there was plenty of space in the warehouse once Grove sales slowed. At this point, with an excess of storage space, the company reached out to its contacts – mainly those who had once been Macmillan graduate trainees and were dotted across the industry, and so came to an agreement with Nigel Newton for Macmillan Distribution to handle Bloomsbury's logistics.

One morning, while going through some finance reports, I was startled to see that the number of employees in Swansea was going through the roof. On investigation, it seemed that Bloomsbury had a new book series that was selling at an unprecedented rate, and that the company was requesting more and more capacity from us. It was the first time I had ever heard of Harry Potter and discovered that Macmillan, by good fortune, had become an early beneficiary of the phenomenon. And so was Swansea's economy, as we took on more warehouse space and hired more people to ship copies around the country.

So nobody knows anything and there is a good deal of luck in publishing as with everything else – but the best editors are always alert to opportunities and ready to act, wherever they may arise. This was certainly the case with Jeffrey Archer. In the summer of 2001, the politician and best-selling novelist was found guilty of having lied during his famous 1987 libel case involving the prostitute Monica Coghlan, and was sentenced to four years in prison – one of the longest ever sentences for perjury in British history. Immediately after this, Harper Collins cancelled their contract with him on the grounds of late delivery of a manuscript, which is obviously a common enough occurrence, but gave them the pretext they needed to distance themselves from a man now regarded as a public disgrace. They were by no means alone – the Conservative Party and Marylebone Cricket Club were highly critical, and a principal concern of government and much of the media at the time was how he might be stripped of his peerage.

With Archer in prison and out of contract, the head of trade publishing at Macmillan, Adrian Soar, saw his chance and went to visit him at the open prison in Lincolnshire where, after an initial stretch in Belmarsh, he was serving his sentence. It was there that they did the deal for his three-volume memoir, *The Prison Diaries* – the complication being that, as it is unlawful to profit from a crime, we were unable to offer him an advance. Always prolific and with little to distract him, Archer wrote the entire memoir while in prison. The first volume, which came out while he was still behind bars, was a tremendous success, and with the additional help of a serialization arrangement with *The Daily Mail*, extremely profitable – though for legal reasons, Archer was unable to fully benefit from this, and all of his earnings had to be restricted to royalties once he was released.

After Archer came out of prison, I was asked to meet him at his penthouse flat on London's South Bank. He had clearly been briefed by someone and began by saying: "I gather you think that fiction is a waste of time, and that science is more important than stories." But he was reassured when I told him that, as a publisher, it wasn't stories or science, but the sales that mattered. We quickly agreed a further deal and, still cross at having been dropped by HarperCollins when at his lowest ebb, he moved all of his backlist over to Macmillan. Archer's total works have sold more than 300 million copies worldwide and over the next twenty years, he probably earned the company something in the region of £2 million profit a year. As I got to know him better, I persuaded him to start writing a blog and that helped to bring in a younger generation and develop a global readership – most notably in India, which has become his biggest market, and where there is little interest in his travails with the British criminal justice system.

MANAGERIAL DIVERSIONS

One of the things about managing a publishing company, or in fact probably any company, is that the things you end up spending most time on aren't necessarily the most profitable. Under the stewardship of Annette Thomas, Nature Publishing Group was going from strength to strength, and I had little reason to interfere. But there were plenty of other things to keep me busy.

Something which took up a fair amount of time was trying to repatriate Macmillan's name in the US. There was, as ever, a long and tortuous history to this. Back in the 1870s, an editor called George Brett opened Macmillan's first office in New York and then, some decades later, bought the US operation from the family, keeping the Macmillan brand name. The Brett family stayed in control of Macmillan in the US right up until the 1960s before undertaking a series of mergers that eventually led to the company ending up in the hands of Robert Maxwell. As part of the untangling of debts and breaking apart of assets in the wake of his chaotic death, the Macmillan name somehow came into the possession of Pearson. In the meantime, back in the 1950s, Macmillan had actually re-entered the US market but, with its name already taken, had had to do so under the name St Martin's Press.

All of this wasn't much of an issue for the management team at St Martin's Press, but the family and board had decided it was time to rectify the situation. In the fifteen years they had owned it, Pearson had done nothing with the Macmillan brand, but as it was worth something to us it meant that it was worth something to them, and I had to spend a considerable amount of 2007 in negotiations with their chief executive Marjorie Scardino, before agreeing to pay a substantial sum for little more than the name. The US and Worldwide companies remained separate operations but it meant that, after a century, all of our businesses could be reunited once again under the Macmillan brand.

There were many other distractions from the day-to-day job of trying to make money through publishing. In the mid-1990s Picador had had a huge success with *Bridget Jones's Diary* and some years later a film version was made. Given that the eponymous heroine works in the publicity department of a publishing company, it seemed natural that Picador would have to provide an internship for the star Renée Zellweger who wanted to spend some time familiarising herself with the British publishing industry and practise her English accent. As ever with Hollywood, the emphasis on secrecy bordered on the hysterical and no one other than the publicity director Camilla Elworthy and me were allowed to know that the new intern was Zellweger, under the pseudonym of Bridget Cavendish, who was in the office doing the photocopying. None of our editorial team seemed to recognise her. We would probably have succeeded in keeping the whole thing under wraps if she hadn't turned up for work every morning in a chauffeur-driven limousine, before having a goodbye embrace with her then boyfriend Jim Carrey. But it was, of course, well worth it – the film tie-in edition of *Bridget Jones's Diary* helped to further boost sales of a series that has sold millions worldwide.

My job at Macmillan was made easier in one significant respect – the company was owned, via Holtzbrinck Publishing Group, by a family. Although the 'supermisery board' had to be endured, public shareholder relations which can take up so much time were not something I had to worry about. However, there was one exception. We had a controlling stake in Macmillan India, which was a publicly listed company on the Madras Stock Exchange. This meant that, for the first time in my career, I had to front an AGM to shareholders. It was actually a less gruelling experience than I had been expecting – apart from obviously wanting bigger dividends, most of the questions from shareholders were about the quality of the 'tiffin', or snacks, being served at the meeting. From what I gather, this seems to be standard at all Indian AGMs and at least it was a better question than the perennial one we had at Bloomsbury in which, long after the series had finished, someone without fail would ask when the next Harry Potter would be coming out.

It was around this time that Sara Lloyd, then Macmillan's head of publicity and the latest in the long line of brilliant gradate recruits, suggested that I do a CEO newsletter for all staff. I thought that if I do anything for staff it would be very boring or else, if at all revelatory, leaked to the rest of the industry. So Sara and I agreed that instead I would do a daily blog, try and keep it interesting and accept it would be public. Every single day for two years I would write something, much to the exasperation of my family and, I suspect, many of my colleagues. Apart from anything else, it was a good way to learn about new media and metrics and what triggered a response. Mentioning celebrity writers didn't get me anywhere, there was too much of that elsewhere, but controversy, provocation and heated argument seemed to work very well. The internet, as the world knows all too well, can be a very angry place and my various tirades against technology companies, literary agents, politicians and regulators were far more effective than I ever imagined in generating traffic. It is perhaps no surprise that, as soon as I left, the blog was disabled.

After ten years at Macmillan, a report showed that, over the decade, the group had generated total post-tax cash of just over £400m. In other words, Dieter had got all of his money back from the acquisition, and the family now had a company worth at least £2bn. It seemed a good time to leave – Macmillan was in good health, it had got back its name in the US, and by this point Stefan was head of Holtzbrinck Publishing Group, with his own clear ideas around the future of media and technology. As ever, when it comes to career decisions the important thing is who you will be working with, rather than what you will actually be doing – in this respect, publishing is probably the same as every other industry, and I still had the enduring lesson I had taken from my time at Harvard – to try and focus on the things in business you most enjoy.

Over the years, I had got to know Nigel Newton and was sure he was someone I could happily work with. He had co-founded Bloomsbury Publishing at the age of 30 and we had frequently crossed paths. The extent to which it really was Nigel (and his young daughter) who had been determined to sign up J.K. Rowling is lost in publishing folklore, but he was an instinctive, incessant and often brilliant deal maker. The distribution partnership between Macmillan and Bloomsbury which had dispatched so many Harry Potter books around the country had worked very well for both companies, and in the course of this I knew he was someone I could trust and work with. And so, in the autumn of 2007, I moved over. There was no acrimony at all in leaving and it came as something of a surprise to colleagues. So much so, that a bemused literary agent on hearing the news, was overheard to ask: "Why is Richard moving to Bloomsbury? I thought he was perfectly happy living in Chelsea."

CHAPTER EIGHT: MAKING BLOOMSBURY LESS MAGICAL

Trying to get off the Harry Potter roller-coaster; going on a spending spree; a publishing love-affair; still trying to get digital right; the sad decline of the British public library service; the culture of Bloomsbury and the feminization of publishing; progress on workforce diversity; marketing and design, and the demise of sales conferences.

When I started at Bloomsbury Publishing it was in a highly unusual position and facing a fascinating challenge. The release in the summer of 2007 of the final volume in the Harry Potter series, *Harry Potter and the Deathly Hallows*, had been a global media event. Bookshops around the country had opened at midnight and the book had broken all records, selling 15 million hardback copies in the first 24 hours, with 2.7 million in Britain alone. The revenues from this obviously made up an outsized part of Bloomsbury's turnover that year, as had been the case for much of the previous decade. The company's income for 2007 had been £150 million, up from £75 million the year before, while in 2005 (also the year of a new Harry Potter release) it had been £110million, and the year before that £84million. But the rollercoaster ride was coming to an end.

Contracting the unknown Joanne Rowling in 1996 to write a seven-book series had been one of the great publishing decisions of all time. The story has been often told of how she was rejected by a dozen publishers before Bloomsbury offered her a small initial advance of £2500 with the agreement that she use initials instead of her first name. This meant that, once the initial series had been published, the scope for future income might have been limited. It was expected that paperback sales would continue but real growth for the company would need to come from elsewhere.

Founded in 1986, Bloomsbury had been a publicly listed company since 1994, and while its share price had been as high as 350p per share a few years previously, it had fallen to around 110p in 2008 when I joined. The company had recently issued a profit warning and analysts fretted that the success of Harry Potter could not be sustained. Despite the pessimism about future profits, the company had accrued £70 million in cash over the decade. It was a nice problem to have, but still a problem – what to do with it? The City expected the reserves to be either paid out in dividends or else strategically invested in growing the company. Confidence hadn't been helped by Bloomsbury paying out some over-generous author advances – including £400,000 for the politician David Blunkett's memoirs, which barely sold more than *The Anatomy of the Dromedary* and, in an auction, more than a £1m for the pop star Gary Barlow's autobiography. Many more of these, and the cash stockpile would dwindle while London's literary agents, well aware of how much money was in the bank, might have seen Bloomsbury as a soft touch.

Our view on all this was clear: Harry Potter was something that came along once in a hundred years, and it wasn't a viable strategy to try and recreate this success. We needed to build a more stable publishing business, and that meant expanding out of purely trade books. I should say this was hardly a unique perspective, and the trends were there for anyone to see if they were following the industry closely enough. The consumer book market, in the UK at least, was failing to grow, Amazon and high street retailers were becoming more powerful and demanding ever larger discounts, while agents were insisting on constraining the rights granted to publishers. If we were going to avoid being squeezed, we had to seek out other parts of the sector.

Fortunately, we had already laid the foundations for this, because back in 2002 Nigel Newton had shrewdly acquired A&C Black. This two-hundred-year-old British company, based in Edinburgh for much of its history but then later in London, had published Walter Scott and P.G Wodehouse, but was best known for its natural history and reference works, including the well-established *Who's Who* and *Writers' and Artists' Yearbook*. It also published *Reeds Nautical Almanac* and some other maritime titles that had once upon a time been published by Harrap. Before I joined, Bloomsbury had also acquired Methuen's drama list, and so again there was the basis for diversification and a move away from trade books.

So we used the Harry Potter bonanza to invest further in companies as well as book advances. Over the next five years we went on a lively corporate acquisition strategy – constantly scouring the industry for potential acquisitions, and always ready to move quickly when opportunities arose. The largest of these purchases, about £20m in total, was for Continuum. In many ways, this company was everything that Bloomsbury wasn't. Although they did have a small and rather eclectic general book list, it was an amalgamation of small academic publishers, mainly in the humanities and social sciences: linguistics, film and music studies, education, and theology books. There were few star authors and no culture of large advances – just a range of solid companies and imprints that had built up a reputation and editorial expertise in distinct markets. Continuum was brought under the new imprint Bloomsbury Academic, along with Bristol Classical Press, which we bought from Duckworth, and added to this was Berg – an academic visual arts company based in Oxford, and which had become a leading publisher of scholarly works in the fields of fashion, design and cultural studies.

It wasn't just academic publishing. We also acquired Osprey, which specialized in military history and had built up a reputation over fifty years on the basis of its illustrations, maps and full-colour photographs. We bought Wisden Cricketers' Almanack, which was a source of particular personal pleasure as well as having intriguing growth prospects, and also Absolute Press, which had pioneered TV tie-in food publishing with Keith Floyd in the early 1980s. As a result of this, the chef Tom Kerridge would become, after J.K. Rowling, one of Bloomsbury's most successful authors.

In 2009 we bought the Arden Shakespeare. This had been owned by International Thomson for many years, as a member of the Thomson family had had a personal attachment to the series. But eventually, the company sold it along with their college textbook interests to an American education operation, Cengage Learning, owned by a private equity group. Not fully understanding that Arden had been revered by generations of

English literature scholars and students, Cengage had managed to get into a high-profile row with one of its editors, sacking a renowned professor who had been labouring for ten years on a new edition of *A Midsummer Night's Dream*. As a result, they incurred the wrath of the international Shakespeare studies community – an online petition in the editor's defence was circulating, and there were even threats of a boycott of all Arden titles if she was not reinstated. I met the distraught Cengage chief executive at Frankfurt Book Fair and, after giving him my commiserations at the bar, offered to take Arden off his hands. We quickly did the deal, and were able to pacify the Shakespeare world by reuniting Arden with Methuen, who had been the original nineteenth century publisher of the series.

We were similarly opportunistic when we moved into legal publishing. We had acquired Hart Publishing, and Tottel, a law and tax publisher that had been spun out of Butterworth. This allowed Bloomsbury to engage in a profitable deal with RELX's (formerly Reed Elsevier) Lexis Nexis who were forced by the Competition and Markets Authority to sell off the Family Law division of their recently-acquired Bristol-based law publisher, Jordan's. It was hard for them to sell to anyone but Bloomsbury as any other large law publisher (such as Thomson or Wolters-Kluwer) would face the same competition issues. The price paid by RELX reflected their predicament and was thus favourable to Bloomsbury.

In terms of subject or market, there was nothing much in common between any of these deals, but that didn't mean there wasn't an underlying strategy. In all cases, the aim was to acquire leading publishers in niche markets, producers of high-quality titles, with subscription revenues wherever possible and good potential for digital growth. A key factor in acquiring Berg, for instance, was that it enabled us to launch the Berg Fashion Library (now Bloomsbury Fashion Central): an online collection of photographic images and content which is now the primary resource for research in fashion and dress. As with most acquisition-based strategies not all these ventures worked immediately but the great advantage in building up a diverse portfolio, was that they didn't all need to. The idea was to get to the point where risk was manageable, and we were no longer dependent on a single author, series or even market. Over the decade, Bloomsbury evolved from being a general book publisher into being a global multi-market publisher, and the share price steadily moved back up.

And of course, we still had Harry Potter. When J.K. Rowling decided that she would be taking her first adult novel to another publisher, we held a meeting with her agent and he agreed that, as our marketing team had long desired, Bloomsbury could launch a new series of illustrated editions of the books. The award-winning illustrator, Jim Kay, was selected by Rowling herself and, like the original series, a new book is released every two or three years. They have proved to be hugely popular – just as the marketing people had foreseen, those who had grown up with the books the first time around were eager to buy the new editions for their families. And this time, when it came to the illustrations, we made sure we had the worldwide rights – including the US.

WISDEN – A LONG-RUNNING LOVE AFFAIR

Probably the acquisition at Bloomsbury closest to my heart was Wisden Cricketers' Almanack. The 'bible of cricket' had been founded by the retired cricketer John Wisden in 1864 and has been published uninterrupted ever since, making it the world's longest-running sports annual. Beloved by collectors, early editions of the almanack sell for many thousands of pounds, while a complete set, on the rare occasion that it comes up for auction, sells for six figures. There is even a business entirely dedicated to the buying and selling of vintage copies.

Its publishing history was, as ever, a complex one. After leaving the Wisden family, it had been owned by Grays-Nicolls, a manufacturer of cricket and sports equipment, before coming (via British Printing Corporation) into the hands of Robert Maxwell, who had all kinds of ideas for it that thankfully never came to pass. In the early 1990s, it came up for auction and I was eager to buy it on behalf of Reed International Books, but once it became clear that the other bidders included the billionaire John Paul Getty Jnr we swiftly dropped the idea. Son of the oil tycoon, Paul was a well-known anglophile and philanthropist who, on being introduced to cricket by Mick Jagger, became one its greatest devotees. He would go on to fund a new stand at Lord's and construct a wonderful ground at his Wormsley Park estate that hosted touring national teams. If he really wanted Wisden, then very little was going to stop him having it.

Getty may have loved cricket, but he had never shown much interest in publishing and, having now acquired a publishing business, he had to find some people to help manage it. Fortunately, Wisden was the kind of institution that easily attracted friends and, although I had failed to buy it for Reed, I was happy to become a non-executive director. Given what was really a very small operation, we were able to pull together a very high-powered board – including the banker and cricketer Matthew Fleming and the magazine publisher John Brown (son of the old OUP publisher, Sir John Brown). At meetings in Getty's flat overlooking Green Park were not just publishers but leading financiers and cricket writers, all of whom were brought together by a love of the game and a willingness to give their time freely to a publishing institution. Over the years, the Wisden Group became an interesting collection of interests. As well as the almanack itself, it also owned *The Cricketer* monthly magazine, *The Oldie* magazine founded by Richard Ingrams, the Cricinfo website and the Hawk-Eye technology system that is widely used in tennis, cricket and other sports to track the trajectory of a ball and assist umpire decisions.

After Paul Getty's death, his son Mark became Chairman. After a strategy meeting at Wormsley Park in 2008, the board discussed whether its future was as a sports entertainment business, with the strengths in editorial and data complementing sports television content, or something else. Mark had already successfully founded the Getty Images photo library, but he didn't have the stomach to start a broadcasting company and acquire sports rights. So instead, he prudently went on a disposal spree, selling Cricinfo to ESPN and *The Cricketer* to BSkyB, with the Hawk-

Eye system later sold to Sony. That just left the almanack itself. After first considering an auction, Mark decided that he couldn't face the furore if it was bought by anyone unsuitable, or too obviously American. And so, twenty years after I had failed to buy Wisden for Reed International, we did a deal so that it could come into the welcoming arms of Bloomsbury.

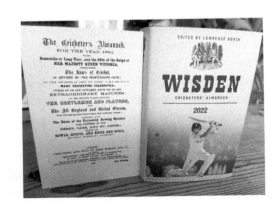

A reprint of the Wisden and a more recent incarnation

Through Bloomsbury, we looked to grow it. It has licensed its brand to Cricket Properties Ltd, a digital content and sponsorship company, which runs Wisden.com. But more importantly, the original almanac still comes out annually, just as it has done every year since 1864, and in April at the start of the season, some 30,000 copies of the distinctive yellow hardback are bought by cricket followers around the world. My heart still leaps when mine arrives.

BECOMING A DIGITAL PUBLISHER IN A DIGITAL WORLD

When I arrived at Bloomsbury, e-books were only just becoming something to think about – Amazon's Kindle was launched in 2007 and Sony's equivalent in 2008. We didn't actually have the digital files of many of our own titles, and began work with Microsoft on the process of digitizing the backlist. As for the rights, it was complicated to say the least. Many were silent on digital rights and hardly any defined what royalty should be paid on e-book sales.

It was now more than twenty-five years since I had negotiated that first OUP dictionary deal with Dictronics. There was a better understanding of electronic publishing broadly but there had been many mis-steps along the way. Part of the difficulty was that some of the very best and most valuable publishing businesses and assets turned out to be the ones most readily destroyed by the internet. The *Encylopedia Britannica* is a well-known instance of this, with its illustrious two-hundred-year-old history counting for very little once Wikipedia arrived. Something similar happened in the early 1990s after Reed acquired the Official Airlines Guide from Maxwell Communication's administrators for £280m. At the time, this was regarded by many as something of a bargain, and was considerably less than Maxwell himself had paid for it just a few years previously – ever since 1929, it had been an extremely profitable publisher of timetables, flight schedules and travel information for airlines. But in the digital age, this information was no longer restricted to a single publisher, and could be made freely available. By 2014, Reed Elsevier had given up on the Official Airlines Guide and agreed to a management buyout.

Of course, Amazon had now become a major force in both print and digital sales. In 2009, Bloomsbury and Amazon had a disagreement over trading terms and they removed the 'buy button' from our titles. They still listed the book, but you could only buy copies from third parties rather than Amazon themselves. The issue was resolved and there was nothing in itself new about this – publishers and retailers had been battling over terms of trade for as long as there have been bookshops. Back in the 1990s, WH Smith had briefly refused to sell any of Heinemann's titles. When I warned the broadcaster and business guru John Harvey-Jones that this meant his latest book would not be on their shelves, he told me not to fold on any account – we didn't, and things were soon settled.

What was, and is, qualitatively different about Amazon is the enormous range of things they do, and therefore the ways in which they can potentially have a stranglehold on you. Ultimately, all that chains such as WH Smith or Blackwell could ever do was threaten not to stock a publisher's books, but Amazon can also refuse to make them available on Kindle, to take the audio version off Audible, to remove their Print on Demand function, or even restrict them from the AbeBooks market place or the Goodreads online reading community. It is only because Amazon is well aware of its enormous power, and mindful of drawing the attention of politicians or regulatory authorities, that its actions are circumscribed – the last thing it needs is a row with governments over bookselling, now such a small part of their overall business. In fact, at the time of writing, Amazon's terms of trade are actually less onerous than some large terrestrial bookselling chains. But it is an unhealthy situation for the online routes to the reading public to be so dominantly controlled by a single company.

PUBLIC LIBRARY ONLINE: TRYING TO MODERNISE LIBRARY SERVICES

One of the more ambitious, if ultimately unsuccessful, experiments in my time at Bloomsbury was Public Library Online – a belated attempt to help protect and modernise the British library service. Like so many others of my generation, I grew up with libraries. They were a formative part of my childhood and introduction to reading. As a young boy, every Saturday morning after swimming, my mother would take me to the local library to choose a book. Later I would study for my O Levels using the textbooks in the Swiss Cottage library. Having been raised in London, there were plenty of examples from not only the great Victorian era of library building, but also the twentieth century as first public subscriptions and then municipal governments provided the funds for libraries across the city. In the East End, places like the old Whitechapel Library had been the means by which working class people and immigrants had been able to educate themselves and progress.

For many decades, public libraries had been a crucial element of the trade publishing landscape. The backbone of fiction publishing for normal, non-bestselling books was the public library system and the UK's four thousand or so branches that sustained much of hardback fiction. In the 1970s, if you published a new detective novel by a decent, middling writer you might print 5000 copies of which as many as 2000 would be sold to the public libraries. There is a generation of writers who were able to build up a readership and earn a living in this manner. In 2007, J.K. Rowling was breaking all sales records, but she was only the 43rd most borrowed author in Britain's public libraries, far behind the likes of lesser-known writers such as Josephine Cox, Ian Whybrow and Katie Flynn. When I was at Reed, there was still a dedicated library sales person selling unbound sheets for library versions of books with reinforced binding to withstand the greater handling.

But the importance of public libraries for publishing and for authors has sadly been in continual decline over the course of my career. There are numerous reasons for this, and not all of them are a cause of regret. The emergence and expansion of Waterstone's in the 1980s and then Amazon since the late 1990s, made it so much easier for people to find and buy books around the UK. Until then, in many small towns across the country, a well-stocked public library (or even a mobile library that came out to villages) was the only way that people could get easy access to a decent selection of books.

But for much of the half century, the major problem has been not just the efficiency of the service, but the level of public funding. This has been particularly acute over the last ten years when libraries have been at the frontline of austerity cuts – their funding has fallen by a third since 2010 and some 800 library branches across the country have shut. The provision of library services is a statutory requirement of local authorities and therefore their responsibility, rather than national government, to manage and fund. This was made clear to me by David Lammy who back in the 2000s was the culture minister responsible for libraries – to which I couldn't help but wonder why he was being paid to be minister for something he claimed to have no control over. Without sufficient championing at either the national or local level, there are now many towns without a functioning public library. Not only has the overall funding been reduced, but so has the proportion that libraries actually spend on books. Many of the country's libraries are Victorian buildings, and often of historical significance, with the unfortunate consequence that more of the budget has had to be spent on repairs, maintenance, conservation and heating rather than stock. It has been estimated that the number of books across the UK's public libraries as whole has fallen from more than 100 million to 75 million since 2005.

The Public Library Online initiative was an attempt to address some of these challenges. It was 2010, Amazon had launched the Kindle in the UK while the new government was about to unleash severe funding cuts on local government. But there was no real idea how public libraries were going to adapt to e-books, and what role they could potentially play in delivering a better and more cost-efficient service. The idea that we developed at Bloomsbury was essentially to take the academic journal model established for university libraries, and apply it to public ones. Instead of purchasing copies of individual titles, libraries would be able to take out a subscription (say £500 per year) with a publisher, giving its members access to e-book versions of some or all the titles that a publisher had released, or had the rights to. Users would be able to use their library card and associated identification details to read a certain number of electronic books a month. It would help libraries to modernize and to serve their members, without the handling or storage costs of physical books. It would be relatively inexpensive and hassle free and the publishers and authors would still get some income from the library system.

But just because you've got a good idea, it doesn't mean it will work. We did manage to get some local authority library services to sign up, including Westminster and Essex, but the spending cuts were so deep that getting libraries to engage on anything other than cost-cutting had become difficult. It would have really benefited from a national licence to stimulate uptake, but for all the meetings with enthusiastic ministers, the British government was incapable of making it happen. This is in contrast to the Dutch Library Service who we succeeded in licensing the service to, and who still run something similar. Part of the problem was that the technology was still quite clunky, and all we could initially offer to libraries was PDF versions of our books, rather than the more flexible formats that work on the range of mobile devices that followed. But the real problem was that, unlike with academic publishing, we couldn't persuade enough other publishers to join as there was a prevailing fear that digital access to ebooks in public libraries would cannibalize book sales. To have really transformed online library service we needed industry-wide partnerships and a number of large trade publishers on board.

And so, despite the excellence and energy of its manager, Public Library Online fizzled out. Public libraries have continued to decline and, over the last fifty years, have demonstrated rather less capacity for change and innovation than the publishing industry. For instance, when print-on-demand arrived, libraries could have helped with the technology's roll-out. Recognising that they didn't have to stock every book, or use laborious and costly inter-library lending systems, they could have offered the option of printing copies there and then. But instead, the reaction of librarians was almost universally one of resistance.

Nor has there been much in the way of enterprise. It doesn't seem

The sad gates of my local public library

unreasonable that libraries could do more to earn at least some revenue themselves – galleries, museums and other cultural institutions, and even leisure centres, have mostly developed a mixed economy model, with a combination of public funding, donations, some paid-for services and other commercial activities, such as a restaurant, gift shop or coffee bar. Almost uniquely, a public library is a place where the public can take out books for free, without being offered much else – free or otherwise.

But ultimately, a flourishing public library system will always depend upon governments or philanthropic foundations with the wisdom to properly fund it. The Mildmay Library round the corner from my home was built in the 1950s, has a colourful post-modern façade and in the 1980s was one of the country's first libraries with a computerised stock management system, but is now in a very sad state and currently open just two and a half days a week. Andrew Carnegie provided the money to found more than six hundred libraries in Britain – the technology billionaires of our current industrial era are unlikely to do the same.

THE CULTURE OF BLOOMSBURY AND INDUSTRY PROGRESS

The four founders of Bloomsbury in 1986 included Liz Calder, the legendary editor who had also helped to found the Groucho Club and the Orange Prize for Fiction. In its early years, before the Harry Potter phenomenon had taken it to unforeseen places, Liz had helped Bloomsbury establish a reputation as a high-quality literary publishing house, publishing the likes of Margaret Atwood and Michael Ondaatje and regularly competing for the Booker Prize.

Although Liz had left by the time I joined and the company had grown considerably, the culture she had established was very much still there, and this included the prominent roles taken by women – not least, Alexandra Pringle who was a superb editor-in-chief for twenty years. Across the company as a whole, probably 70% of the staff were female during my time there. This was a reflection on Bloomsbury, but also how the overall culture of publishing had changed over the years – according to the Publishers Association's most recent survey, women now occupy just over half of the industry's senior management positions. Of course, this reflects broader changes in the workplace and society, but the industry has also taken steps on its own accord. For instance, the Kim Scott Walwyn Prize, named in honour of the brilliant editor at OUP, was founded after her death and has been awarded to 'exceptional women in publishing' since 2003.

Despite the progress, it has not always been straightforward. Take the instance of The Society of Bookmen, which had been founded in the 1920s as a monthly dining club for professionals from across the book trade, bringing together publishers, booksellers, printers, librarians and the occasional author. The dinners, held at the Savile Club in Mayfair, had long been an important part of London's publishing scene – a place to socialise and do business, and for younger publishers to learn and make contacts. Forty years into its existence, the Society had belatedly admitted women in 1972, and I joined in 1988 shortly after I started at Reed. But by the 21st century, with 40% of the members being female, many felt that the name 'Bookmen' was increasingly problematic. There had been two attempts to get it changed, but it required at least two thirds of the members to vote for change in a ballot and had failed to pass. In desperation, the chair of the Society called an emergency motion at one of the monthly dinners and, in a show of hands held there and then, it was renamed The Book Society.

I had been at this dinner and obviously voted for the change of name, but was troubled by the use of an emergency motion as a way of avoiding a full democratic ballot and submitted my resignation to the Society's management committee. Instead, as is the way of things, I accepted their suggestion that I should become president of The Book Society and work with the chair to help ensure that principles of good governance were upheld in the future. A couple of years after this, a member of the Society pointed out that membership of the Savile Club where we regularly dined was restricted to men, and so an unsuitable host venue. I spoke with the Club manager who confirmed that this was the case and was unlikely to change in the foreseeable future – their only female member being someone who had joined as a male and then subsequently undergone a sex change! And so we moved to the Conduit, a club in Covent Garden. It was a shame to end the long association that the Society had enjoyed with the Savile Club but also, I strongly believed, the right thing to do.

It was a small but symbolic mark of how far publishing had progressed. We should never be complacent, but when I look back over the last fifty years, the progress has been astonishing and hugely positive. When I had been at Pergamon in the mid-1970s, there had still been an annual "Miss Pergamon" contest. As announced in the staff paper, the *Pergamon Gazette,* in August 1974, this wasn't the "usual kind of beauty contest" and the judges were "looking for other qualities as well, such as personality, poise, confidence and efficiency." The winner would receive a weekend holiday in Paris, a new wardrobe and a "titled sash, cloak and crown" which would be needed for when she greeted VIP visitors and was in attendance at official company events. Pergamon, it should be borne in mind, was an Oxford-based scientific publisher that at the time was considered one of the most forward-thinking and dynamic publishing companies in the UK.

As well as more women working in publishing and in more senior roles, another positive development is the increased diversity of the workforce. The Publishers Association has done excellent work over the years promoting change and tracking progress on the make-up of the workforce in terms of women and also minority groups. According to a recent survey, representation from non-white ethnic groups now stands at 15% of the industry and while more can be done (especially in terms of socio-economic backgrounds), the improvement over fifty years is startling. Of course, back in the 1970s no one thought to collect the kind of workforce data that we have now, but you didn't need data to know there were serious problems.

Even if well intentioned, I can recall moments of some discomfort from the time. Before I joined OUP in 1975, I was contacted by Bill Patchett, the company's first ever Personnel Director, who wanted to meet for a drink before I started. We went for a couple of cheerful pints in a pub in East Oxford in the course of which he kindly advised me to start work on March 31 instead of the beginning of April, as I would notch

> **ARE YOU "MISS PERGAMON" 1974-5?**
>
> We're out to find "Miss Pergamon 1974-5" from all the members of "The Colophon Clan" and what a lucky girl she will be when she is voted her title by the readers of the "Pergamon Gazette"!
>
> No! We are not offering film or television tests as prizes — that's "Cloud 9 Scene" — but something more realistic and down to earth ... "A weekend in Paris for Two", Plus a new wardrobe for the trip, "Spending Money", a titled sash, cloak and crown. Plus the responsibility of greeting V.I.P. visitors when appropriate and being in attendance at certain exhibitions in which the Company participates from time to time.
>
> [You have the responsibility of choosing your partner for the trip, but the Company will accept no responsibility for the consequences!]
>
> Make no mistake about it this is NOT the usual kind of "Beauty Contest" as such, for as 'they' say "Beauty is only skin deep". We are looking for other qualities as well, such as personality, poise, confidence and efficiency — and when we find her she will deserve her title. — "Miss Pergamon 1974-5".
>
> All you have to do to enter — and it is entirely free — is to send the Editor a photograph of yourself only — wearing either day, evening or bathing wear and on the reverse side add the following information:
> Name:
> Vital Statistics:
> Department:
> Position:
> Int. Tel. No.:
> Interests or hobbies:
> Your ambition:
>
> In each of the following issues of the "Pergamon Gazette" the Judging Panel — (Will all male members of the staff queue up on the left please!) will publish a selection of candidates and upon which, readers will be asked to send in their votes on a POSTCARD ONLY please — and state in no more than 30 words why they are voting for that person.
>
> The Finals will take place just before Christmas, and the winner will be chosen and crowned at the Company's Christmas Party, so that "Miss Pergamon 1974-5" will hold her title until December 1975. They say "Paris in the Spring" is a joy to behold ... so will our Miss Pergamon be too! Where are you? In which department do you work?
>
> SEND IN YOUR PHOTOGRAPH - TODAY!
>
> "UP AND AWAY"—AND THOSE "SUMMER SHOTS"
> Go through your holiday photos today — for we are sure you will find one that will come under one of the
>
> PERCENTAGE TO EFFORT MEANS GREATER EFFICIENCY!
> 100%...I did.

Sexism at work

up another year's pension – something that I still benefit from today. Bill then asked me, in a perfectly friendly way, if I was Jewish, and when I told him I was, he tried to reassure me: "Don't worry, you'll be fine. There's one other of your lot here." The 'one other' turned out to be Andrew Schuller, who happened to have a German surname and, despite having a Jewish father, has never identified as being Jewish. And so I was the only Jew at OUP.

Some thirteen years later, on this occasion on the brink of my leaving OUP, I was contacted by Martin Jacomb, who was then chair of the investment bank, Kleinwort Benson and sat as an external director on the Finance Committee of OUP. Over lunch at his club, Martin made a half-hearted attempt to persuade me to stay. I was interested as to why he, somebody I hardly knew, had been given this task, and he indicated what I had suspected: the board had felt that, as a fellow Jew, he was best placed to get through to me.

All of this is curious, because already by this time British publishing had been shaped by a generation of great Jewish publishers. Chief among these was Paul Hamlyn. On discovering that he had offered me a job, the Vice-Chancellor of Oxford University warned me against going to work with a 'street trader', but he was already by this time one of the key figures in post-war British publishing. What's more, many of his contemporaries had also been Jewish.

In the early 1980s, the Publishers Association had a plan to set up a new digital platform, Publishers Databases Ltd, which would be owned and run by the PA and look to consolidate publishers' electronic publications into a single database, the contents of which would be sold through subscription. We had a meeting in Bedford Square of all the relevant publishers in order to make the key decision as to whether to invest in the venture and hire a chief executive to get it started. When it came to the vote, nineteen of the publishers' representatives voted for the proposal and I alone voted against. Afterwards, Clive Bradley, the chief executive of the PA, queried my vote and I told him that I didn't know of any successful publishing venture that didn't have a strong Jewish element, but in this case there were twenty of us round the table, and I was the only one, and so naturally sceptical. Sure enough, Publishers Databases Ltd never came to anything.

Another, perhaps less remarked upon, aspect of diversity is in terms of the age of the workforce. At Bloomsbury, there were people there of all ages – Alexandra Pringle has only just retired from her illustrious career at the age of 70 and Nigel Newton is still going strong as chief executive in his late 60s. Meanwhile, the indomitable Liz Calder co-founded a new publishing company after Bloomsbury and, in her 80s, was recently a judge on the Booker Prize. Certainly, when I started out at Harrap, one of the things that I never expected was that, at the age of 74, I would still be in publishing. At OUP, one of the main drivers of career opportunity was retirement – senior editors and management would work until they were 65 and no longer (or 60 if you were female). This may well have been related to the generous pensions offered by OUP, but on the whole it is very much for the better that people can keep working if they choose, and that editors as talented as Alexandra and Liz can continue to contribute to publishing.

DESIGN, MARKETING AND SALES

During my time at Bloomsbury, we probably had no more than half a dozen sales reps based in the UK. By contrast, back at Harrap all those years ago there were about ten sales reps for trade and another ten for schools. They represented about a fifth of all staff and were a significant element of the company, the engine for bringing in the money. It was the same for most publishing companies, with some also having university sales reps, who would try to persuade professors and course directors to recommend textbooks to their students and libraries (a pretty tough assignment in most cases). The reps were hired because of their sales expertise and tended to have a commercial background, with hopefully also a bit of literary interest. International sales teams were more likely to be made up of university graduates and multilingual, whereas the UK reps tended to be more purely salesmen (and they were usually men), with good knowledge of their particular patch, and plenty of contacts in the book trade.

The importance of sales reps to a publisher was reflected in its sales conferences. These were the bi-annual company events (for the spring and autumn seasons), which often took place in a hotel or even on occasion at an overseas resort. They would be attended by the reps themselves, editors and publicists with often the senior executives there and star authors who were invited to speak. The idea was for editors to enthuse the reps about forthcoming titles – explain the plots of the novels and so forth, and fire them up so they could all the better go out and sell them to bookshops around the country. I was never sure how helpful these were in improving sales, but they did bring together different parts of the company and were an effective form of bonding, so something has definitely been lost as these events have declined in importance – nowadays, far from gathering in a hotel, they are more often done on Zoom.

The number and importance of sales reps has sadly declined over the last fifty years, and for many reasons. One of them is consolidation. At Reed International, one of the first managerial tasks I had to undertake was to help integrate the various sales teams from Heinemann, Methuen, Mitchell Beazley and the other publishers that had been acquired. The result was that the number of individual sales people was reduced from sixty or seventy to no more than twenty. This reduction has mirrored the consolidation that has taken place amongst retailers. The days when a sales rep would be responsible for a region such as Scotland and spend his days driving around, staying in hotels, racking up expenses and visiting each town's bookshop to take orders have largely gone.

The shop-to-shop sales role has gone, but in some ways, the role has reverted back to its true meaning – it is a company 'representative', someone who represents the publisher and its authors rather than simply selling books. They now more often provide author support: they accompany authors at events, book launches and festivals. They also act as customer service – when a bookshop needs to make an emergency order, or there is a distribution problem or the shop has been put on stop because of credit control, they are the first point of call. So the role has actually enhanced and broadened and I sometimes think they should be considered as regional managing directors – after all, the sales for a particular region of the UK might well exceed that of a small country.

In stark contrast to the decline in sales is the prominence of marketing and the increased size of marketing and publicity teams. When I started at Harrap there was a publicity manager, who also had one or two people working for him to produce catalogues for bookshops, and mailings to schools. There was no marketing director, and I can't recall any input from marketing into my work as an editor. At OUP there were marketing managers, but they sat firmly within the sales teams rather than having their own dedicated department. But at Bloomsbury, as with most publishers today, it would be fair to say that marketing has a much higher status within the company. With the growth in the number of new titles each year and the subsequent inability of bookshops to display more than a fraction of these, publishers need to reach out beyond intermediaries directly to the potential purchaser – not an easy task given the differing interests and locations of book buyers around the world. The internet has made low-cost direct-to-consumer marketing more feasible and the recent success of the TikTok Book Club is an outstanding example. Nonetheless the challenge of finding ways of getting attention for a book, series, or publishing operation has never been more complex, challenging, and potentially rewarding – and this is reflected in the status and salaries of good marketing executives.

Related to this, another significant change has been in the role and growing importance of design. The likes of Paul Hamlyn and Terence Conran had spearheaded high-quality production values thirty years ago, but design has become an essential part of a publishing house like Bloomsbury. We had an excellent art director and in-house team of designers. But such was the emphasis on design that they were rarely allowed to get on with their job and the cover meetings would typically involve dozens of people, in which the poor designer would be run ragged with changes and unhelpful suggestions. For editors especially, the design of a book cover was a primary consideration but it was notable how often senior managers like me, who have little design sense, would feel obliged to have an opinion.

Nor is it just the design of books themselves. Designers, and design values, permeate a modern publisher. Back when I was at Harrap or OUP, things were very different – although the cover design was always regarded as part of the editors' job, I would send off the manuscript to the designers and by and large trust their judgements and good taste.

A large part of the reason for this must again relate to the sheer increase in books being published. The number of new titles released each year in the UK is now not far under 200,000, which is often said to be the highest per capita in the world. Of course, many of these will never be sold to the general public, but the need for a book cover to stand out, and to be eye catching on the shop table and web page has become essential. It is perhaps no wonder then that, along with the plethora of literary prizes and industry galas, there is an increasing number of book cover awards.

CHAPTER NINE: BRITISH PUBLISHING: AN INTERNATIONAL BESTSELLER

From Imperial legacy to global success; Japanese wisdom; the expansion of ELT publishing; the continuous rise of the English language; Bloomsbury goes to Qatar; the challenges and complexities of international diplomacy.

B ritish publishers have always looked for overseas markets to enhance their sales and support their authors outside the home market. Bloomsbury was no exception. Its first overseas office in 1998 was unsurprisingly in New York and launched with a bang and a series of bestsellers including Anna Pavord's *The Tulip* and, a few years later, Susanna Clarke's *Jonathan Strange and Mr Norrell*. It would be from this office that Anthony Bourdain's *Kitchen Confidential* would herald his glittering career.

In 2003, via the acquisition of Berlin Verlag, Bloomsbury established itself in the German-language markets to distribute English-language books and publish in German. In Australia an office was established in Sydney for marketing, sales and distribution, while in Delhi local publishing was encouraged in English and in local languages which included editions of Harry Potter in Bengali, Gujarati, Hindi, Malayalam, Marathi, Tamil, and Telugu. Localised commissioning in India was essential for a market so different from Europe, and in which there is a tradition of self-help books and works by gurus that we had little insight into. For instance, Bloomsbury enjoyed huge success with Shiv Khera, a motivational speaker whose books *You Can Win, You Can Achieve* and *You Can Sell* all becoming bestsellers.

Even at the very beginning of my career, publishing in London was very much an international enterprise. But what has significantly changed is its geography. Harrap & Co was only really international in as much as it served Commonwealth markets (and France with its bilingual dictionaries). It had an office in Australia, usually managed by a less reputable member of family, and up until Indian independence it had had an office in Bombay. We would look to sell into Australia, parts of Africa and India – all former British colonies, while Canada was considered at least as important a market as the US. By contrast, Europe and most of the Middle East meant little to us and Latin America, never mind Japan or China, even less. There was the Frankfurt Book Fair, but other than that I didn't undertake a single visit to a European city (except Dublin) in my time at Harrap.

Back in the early 1970s these Commonwealth markets could still be lucrative ones, and my first business lunch of any consequence was with Dr Yanney Ewusie, biologist and chair of the Nigerian schools examination board. To my delight, I was allowed to charge the lunch to company expenses and we had Chicken Kiev at a restaurant in Covent Garden, most of whose rich buttery content I unfortunately managed to squirt over his tie. Nevertheless, over the meal, we agreed that he would write a tropical biology illustrated guide. It was well worth the cost of lunch and dry cleaning bill: we sold fifty thousand copies, all printed in the UK and shipped over to Nigeria for their secondary schools.

Lucrative deals like these became fewer, but when it came to international markets the Commonwealth still had a tight grip on British publishing until the end of the 1970s, and the situation wasn't very different when I started at Oxford University Press. In the case of OUP, its international networks and markets had been shaped not just by the legacy of the British Empire, but also by the distinct and influential role that Christianity had played in this. As one of the world's most important publishers of Bibles, prayer books and other theological works, its operations were rooted in Anglican countries around the world and these naturally tended to be former British colonies – US, Canada, Australia, parts of West and Southern Africa and also India. As with Harrap, sales into Europe, Latin America, the Gulf or South East Asia, were less significant early in my career there. In fact, according to OUP's financial reporting system, all international sales were organised under two categories or what were called Branches. Branch 1 covered US, Canada, Australia, while Branch 2 covered the rest of the world (of which India and Nigeria were probably the largest markets). It was the Anglosphere and whiteness that dominated overseas strategy and sales.

By contrast, Pergamon had had an entirely different international focus. There was an office in New York, and we were connected across Central Europe, which was where Maxwell had begun his career. In those days, the scientific research coming out of the Soviet Union, in the Russian language, was world-leading, especially in the physical sciences, and Pergamon had the rights to publish much of this work in English. But it also had interests in many of the world's growing markets. Britain's position in the global economy was changing and for entrepreneurs like Maxwell who could sense this, the rewards would be great. In Europe and many other parts of the world, the later twentieth century was still a time of resurgence, with prolonged economic growth, increased academic research and an expansion in higher education. Japan in particular had by this time established itself as a powerhouse in scientific research and, following the catastrophic damage of the Second World War, was rebuilding its universities and restocking its libraries. Maxwell was determined that Pergamon should be at the forefront of meeting this demand.

By the 1980s Japan had become a fabulous market for British books and journals, and a revitalised OUP was starting to reap the benefits. Along with its great expansion of education and the learning of English, the Yen was strong, making imports from the UK relatively affordable. On one occasion when I was there we took an order for 6000 sets of the new edition of the OED, which even with the 33% discount represented a sale of £6 million – alas, OUP didn't wasn't in the habit of paying its staff commission.

Ultimately, international publishing should never just be about trade and markets – it is as much about cultural exchange, learning, friendship and wisdom. The thing I remember best from my visits to Japan is that I frequently had the pleasure of meeting with Hirokawa Medical Publishers in Tokyo to try to sell them translation rights. Despite my youth and the fact that I was doing the selling, Mr Hirokawa, a distinguished older gentleman, treated me with enormous respect, and entertained me in fine restaurants in London and Tokyo. On one visit to his offices, he amazed me by ushering me through various sliding doors into the presence of his father, the founder of the business. This extremely old man was very small with a wispy white Japanese beard seated on a wooden plank and smiling benignly. The translator explained to me that Mr Hirokawa senior was delighted to meet me and wondered if I had any questions for him. The best I could think of at the spur of the moment was: 'Can revered publisher Mr Hirokawa Senior share with me the secret of successful Japanese publishing?" This was translated and there was a long pause before he responded in Japanese. The translator turned to me and said: "Mr Hirokawa Senior says the secret is not to print too many copies." Wise words indeed.

THE GROWTH OF ELT PUBLISHING

Over the last fifty years, the UK Bible business declined inexorably but this decline was more than replaced by the rise of English language teaching and learning. Again, this was particularly the case with OUP. For instance, Spain introduced mandatory teaching of English from the first year at primary school in the early 1970s leading to a demand for English language materials. Most other Western European countries followed similar strategies. In what was seen at the time, not least by me, as a risky and expensive strategy, OUP in the late 70s opened up a network of offices in many European cities, staffed by relatively highly-paid educators and sales agents who worked to develop markets for English language courses and textbooks. The gamble, led by the dynamic Stephen Warshaw, paid off – the Oxford brand, the quality of the management and materials was such as to propel OUP into becoming the world's leading ELT publisher.

It wasn't just Europe – Asia and the Middle East were turning into lucrative markets. A Lebanese gun runner had been ordering copies of OUP's ELT dictionaries as they made the ideal top cover to stack above the weaponry in his crates. Before too long, he realised that the margins on these books was frequently higher than the firearms, and he turned himself into one of the OUP's biggest ELT agents buying English language dictionaries and textbooks until the inevitable falling out.

Meanwhile, a highly gifted publisher named Raymond Ernest Brammah (always known as REB) had opened up an office in Kuala

Lumpur publishing school books and translating works into Bahasa Melayu, the Malay language. As OUP's East Asia manager from 1955 until his retirement in 1990, REB worked tirelessly to publish books and develop relations with librarians and educators across the entire region. Over the course of his long career, he expanded OUP out of the traditional Commonwealth bases of Malaysia, Hong Kong and Singapore to establish offices in Tokyo, Korea, Jakarta and Bangkok.

Something similar was achieved in Latin America by Macmillan. Chris West, one of the company's most talented graduate trainees, had moved to Mexico in 1970s as a sales rep and made it his home. Over the years he steadily built up the ELT business in the region, acquiring companies in Mexico and Argentina. This eventually became Grupo Macmillan Ibero-America, principally a publisher of ELT, but in some markets also maths and science curriculum titles. Alongside Pearson, Oxford and Macmillan, Cambridge University Press was building a huge market share with their textbooks supported by the Cambridge English Qualifications – millions of students around the world studying for Cambridge's qualifications would also purchase their books and learning materials.

The corporate strategy for all publishers has always been – if you manage to develop a presence in ELT in a particular territory, can you then build up curriculum materials and textbooks, and become an all-encompassing education publisher? So Macmillan moved into Argentina, acquiring Estrada, the country's oldest publisher, and Puerto de Palos. This meant that Macmillan became a publisher of primary and secondary textbooks, as well as reference books. Buenos Aires is a great city to locate a publishing company, were it not for the country's periodic politico-economic crises. The businesses there were well structured, with good systems and excellent local staff who produced beautifully designed books.

Doing business in 1990s Latin America certainly had its challenges. In countries such as Mexico, the national government would take a very clear view on what school books were acceptable and tended to strictly control them. Changes of government were therefore disruptive and brought significant changes. A new education minister would often mean a different set of relationships and favored parties, and it was understood textbook providers were part of this. There were other difficulties – Brazil was, after Mexico, the largest market, but business was always difficult, partly because securing government orders seemed to require unspecified extra costs. Another problem was that currency exchange rates could be volatile and so fixing salaries was difficult – inflation would vary wildly at different times and across different countries. In some countries there was also the possibility of adopted school textbooks being stolen form the warehouse by the security guards.

Outside of publishers of a certain generation, the names of Raymond Brammah and Chris West are unsung compared to the literary editors of Central London or Manhattan. But if anyone ever deserved a Queen's Award for Export, then it was them. Their incredible energy and diligence over the years has helped to build up businesses and a network of booksellers, publishers, educators and authors. Millions of English language books, and export earnings for the UK, have been generated off the back of their work. There are plenty of people who have travelled the globe winning orders for British businesses, but these people did something that has had a much more long-term impact – with generation after generation still reading English literature and admiring British culture.

Particular credit must also go to the British Council. Much like the BBC World Service, it is an institution almost perpetually under attack and facing budget cuts from an unimpressed British government while being enormously valued and respected outside of the UK. One of the most effective schemes administered by the British Council was the English Language Book Society, which subsidised textbooks to be sold at around a third of the UK price. The focus was on medicine, life sciences, accountancy, English language and agriculture. The authors were paid a fair royalty and the scheme helped to develop a functioning book trade in these countries. While I was Medical Editor at OUP, we had *Cunningham's Textbook of Anatomy*, the direct competitor to *Gray's Anatomy*, and so we came to a gentleman's agreement with Longman that neither of us would submit our book to the ELBS for India, as whichever one was selected would almost certainly kill off the other in that market. Before this ever came to the attention of the Office of Fair Trading, ELBS was shut down, an early casualty of the Thatcher government's spending cuts. This was a great shame and also short-sighted, as the scheme had greatly helped to build up the demand for high-quality textbooks and gave British publishers (and thus pharmaceutical and other industries) a presence in what, two decades later, would be called emerging markets.

Working in such markets is not without its perils. On one occasion, it was alleged that a Macmillan sales rep in Sudan had 'offered an incentive' in order to help facilitate a government order to supply textbooks. It seemed that this was by no means an unusual practice, but the World Bank had provided educational funds to the Sudanese government and this came to their attention, prompting an investigation by the UK's Serious Fraud Office. Although I had left Macmillan and was at Bloomsbury by this time, I was quizzed in what was, in fifty years of publishing, my only involvement, albeit fleeting, in a criminal investigation. All of my Macmillan emails were searched using the keyword 'commission' – although as I tried to explain to the SFO, this was an extremely common term in publishing, and so it was little wonder that it had produced thousands of results for them to trawl through.

In truth, although I obviously assisted in the investigation, the whole thing was slightly pointless – as I told them after they had finished questioning me. The cost of the case, which was led by corporate lawyers and accountants working for the SFO, far exceeded the trivial amount of the initial bribe which (as far as I could ever gather) seemed to have had something to do with getting access to an education minister through his driver. There seemed to be little appreciation of how hard it is to do business in many of these countries on the same basis as in the UK – as anyone working not just in educational publishing, but pharmaceuticals or healthcare would confirm. The upshot was that Macmillan paid a substantial settlement to the SFO, mainly to cover the costs of its investigation. A number of other publishers also had to make similar settlements. In addition, the World Bank imposed a three-year ban on dealing with Macmillan, so the loss was probably most felt by the students and teachers in Africa who were unable to access the books and materials they needed.

THE DOMINANCE OF THE ENGLISH LANGUAGE

Alongside, and helping to enable, globalisation has been the rise of English as the lingua franca of our era. There are now approximately 1.4 billion speakers of the English language around the world. English is the globe's business language, and therefore the second language for almost everyone. For people in the US and UK, the vast majority of whom have never needed to learn another language, this is a huge inbuilt advantage.

The impact on British publishing has been enormous and often under-appreciated, with native English speakers taking it for granted that this is just how things are, and being notoriously reluctant to learn anyone else's language. The dominance of the English language across Europe is particularly striking. When Bloomsbury released the final title in the Harry Potter series, more than a million copies of the English language hardback were sold in Germany.

English is the business language of the world, but just as significant over the last fifty years has been its unstoppable rise to become the dominant scientific and academic language. In many scientific fields, this represents a major change. Medieval natural philosophers wrote in Latin, and the language of the Enlightenment had been French, but from the late 19th century up until World War II, most of the leading scientific papers and books were written in German, reflecting the extraordinary advances that German-speaking scientists made in this period. This was as true for physics as it was for biology and, especially, chemistry. Up until the mid-20th century, half of the world's scientific literature was written in German and as late as the 1970s it was still the case that chemistry undergraduates in the UK were encouraged to take courses in German. When I was at Pergamon in the mid-1970s, we still published multi-lingual journals – that is journals featuring papers written in languages other than English (principally German) and without translation, but as English became more and more dominant, this practice had all but vanished by the 1980s.

ADVENTURES IN THE GULF

In some respects, it could be said that the role of the UK publishing industry has remained much the same while the world around it has changed radically. All the things that make up the excellence of British publishing – flair, editorial rigour, innovation and risk-taking, high-quality production values, design and marketing talent have always been there. But what is different are the markets, the business opportunities and distribution channels.

A case in point is Bloomsbury's venture in Qatar. It was early 2008 when Sheikha Moza of Qatar met Nigel Newton at a dinner. As the consort to the then Emir of Qatar, she chaired the Qatar Foundation and saw herself as playing a leading role in the educational and cultural development of the emirate and the wider Gulf region. The Qatari state was going through one of its intermittent periods of renewal and openness and, as part of plans to be less dependent on gas revenues, Sheikha Moza wanted Bloomsbury to help build a publishing industry from scratch. While this was going on, her daughter Sheikha Al-Mayassa, was merrily breaking records at auction houses around the world, as she spent hundreds of millions of dollars on artworks to fill the museums and galleries they were building. Meanwhile, other parts of the family were focusing on major sports events, constructing stadiums and landing the football World Cup.

And so with Sheikha Moza's support Bloomsbury Qatar Foundation Publishing was established, with an office in Education City, Doha located near a cluster of international campuses such as Carnegie-Mellon and launched with a glittering event by Her Majesty Queen Elizabeth II at Windsor Castle. It was a curious and, for a while, highly profitable arrangement – the Qatar Foundation owned the company, but licensed the brand name from Bloomsbury and paid a fee to oversee management. The company started with the Arabic translation of Bloomsbury books, and later they were persuaded to found QScience – an open-access journal publishing division for leading scientific research in the Middle East, with the astronaut Buzz Aldrin paid a substantial fee to give the keynote at the launch event.

What had attracted Sheikha Moza was not only our editorial skills and publishing expertise, but also the association with a leading British brand redolent of excellence, in the same way that they had paid good money to attract international universities. In this regard, our name was especially important – it had been a stroke of genius on Nigel's behalf to call his company Bloomsbury. Just as, all those years ago, Walter and Eva Neurath had made the inspired choice to launch their high-end art publishing company with the name Thames & Hudson, even if it did mean that Walter (a Jewish immigrant who had come to London in the 1930s) would be addressed as Mr Hudson for the rest of his career.

As profitable as it was for Bloomsbury, the venture could only last so long. It is a legal requirement that companies based in Qatar must have a minimum proportion of Qatari citizens on the payroll and many of the senior roles had to be occupied by wealthy members of the Qatari elite. It wasn't unheard of for their chauffeurs to turn up at the office, sign in for the day on their behalf, and then promptly leave. For all the strategy meetings we helped to run in Qatar, I never had much confidence that anything would happen as a result of our decisions and, while we did send over good editors to work there, it was hard to get them to stay long. Setting up a publishing company in a dry country presented another challenge: the staff did manage to find a licensed bar at the Four Seasons Hotel, but the prices were outlandish and they were strictly forbidden from charging alcohol on any of their expenses.

Eventually, there was an internal power struggle within Qatar and a different member of the ruling family took charge, resulting in a total change of management. This happened almost overnight, with experienced publishers suddenly finding themselves being overseen by a young Qatari woman. Most of the British staff found the situation impossible and came back to the UK, or else moved to Dubai, where working conditions were easier. The partnership with Bloomsbury formally ended in 2015 and it now continues as the Hamad bin Khalifa University Press, with QScience still running as part of this. But Sheikha Moza's dream of making Qatar a leader in publishing was never realised. There are any number of factors why the UK is a centre for publishing and so many countries around the world aren't – and replicating these is far from straightforward.

INTERNATIONAL DIPLOMACY

While I was at Bloomsbury, at the Frankfurt Bookfair of 2014, I was elected president of the International Publishers Association. Having already served as vice-president, and represented the UK's Publishers Association at the IPA and the Federation of European Publishers (FEP), international relations were something I had experienced, albeit not always enjoyed. My personal priority in my two-year term was to make the IPA much more international. Founded in 1896 in Paris and based in Geneva, for most of its history it had been driven by European and North American interests. By the second decade of the twenty-first century, this was no longer tenable, and the most obvious omission was China – a country which not only wanted to join, but was home to the second biggest publishing market in the world.

There was a considerable amount of opposition to this – and also to Saudi Arabia, who had also applied to join. This was in many ways understandable. Since its inception, the two pillars of the IPA have always been the protection of copyright and the freedom to publish, as a fundamental aspect of the human right to freedom of expression. On the first of these, at least, China had made considerable progress. For the first thirty years of my career, it had been largely ignored by British publishers, both trade and academic, as not much more than a gigantic site for piracy. After the fourth Harry Potter came out, a number of Chinese publishers decided that rather than wait for the rest of the books to be written by J.K Rowling, they would just hire authors to finish the series for them, producing highly eccentric works of literary fantasy. Amusingly, these were then pirated in turn by other Chinese publishers. But a condition of joining the World Trade Organisation in 2001, was that China signed up to the Berne Convention, the international agreement for the protection of literary and artistic works. The Chinese government is nothing if not resolute and, in a very short space of time, China went from largely lawless with regards to intellectual property to highly compliant, with prison sentences of up to ten years for those that infringed copyright.

But on the second IPA pillar – the freedom to publish without censorship – things were (and are) much more problematic, and on this point many of the European publishing associations remained firmly opposed to China, not to mention Saudi Arabia, joining. As is so often the case, however, the size of the markets that these countries offered began to sway minds. It certainly helped that China was prepared to match the contribution of the US, which was the top subscriber.

Several member publishers associations remained opposed, at least in public, when we assembled in Frankfurt in 2015 for our annual assembly. Given the strength of opinion on both sides, I decided to let the discussion run until everyone had had their say. It was a highly intelligent debate, with good arguments made from all sides on the issues of censorship and the nature of freedom to publish. As President, I didn't have a vote myself (unless in the case of a tie), but didn't want to absent myself from the issue and so, at the end, put forward my own opinion, which was that both national organisations should be allowed to join. When it eventually came to the ballot, both the China and Saudi Arabia associations were admitted to membership, bringing in revenue and also increasing IPA's global relevance.

But just because they were now members, the IPA did not by any means give up on its principles. The next year we beefed up the IPA's

Freedom to Publish prize, renaming it the Prix Voltaire, in tribute to the French philosopher and writer, and secured sponsorship so that it is now worth ten thousand Swiss francs each year. It was my great satisfaction to present the inaugural award to Ensaf Haidar, the wife of Raif Badawi, founder of a secularist website in Saudi, who was serving a ten-year sentence under the country's blasphemy laws.

These kinds of debates will forever be at the heart of international relations – as I write, various economic, culture and sports bodies around the world are deciding whether to eject Russia. Spats like this also tend to attract news headlines, but the IPA continues to quietly do good work in the background, with a seasoned chief executive. Located next to WIPO in Geneva, it has a surprisingly small number of paid officers – fewer than five people. But they help ensure that the publishing industries, and writers and businesses that depend upon copyright protection, are represented alongside those (often much larger) interests who derive their value from patents and trademarks. There are authors around the world receiving royalty checks from overseas sales who probably have no idea at all that this is in part because the IPA is defending their interests and protecting their works.

CHAPTER TEN: BEING A MENSCH

Setting up a publishing company; still trying to understand publicity and sales; the role of social media; the science (or art) of modern publishing; still trying to come to terms with agents; the enduring problem of book returns; how to value a publishing company; the ever-changing geography of London publishing; a European publisher in a post–Brexit world

In 2019, for the first time in my career and in the year that I turned 70, I set up my own business. The aim was not to grow a huge business, rather I wanted to publish books in the way I thought it might be possible to, and to see if there were any insights from DIY publishing that I could learn and share. It is still very much a commercial enterprise, and one with no distinct market niche.

Over the years, the cost of discounting from booksellers and the loss of public library orders have made the midlist more difficult and usually overlooked by the bigger publishers, who tend to focus on bestsellers or potential bestsellers, which brings with it the burden of big advances and the danger of a more formulaic mindset. And so I set up Mensch Publishing to try and target the midlist, and to do this with certain business principles. I only publish books with world rights, because as I'd seen so many times before, it was the rights income that equaled much of the profit. I don't offer any advances, but instead pay royalties of 25% on my sales income – that is the actual money received from sales rather than the recommended retail price. I also account quarterly, rather than twice a year, and there are no other delays, so as soon as the money hits my account, I pay 25% to the author. Some agents are comfortable with this and they like the fact that if they submit something that isn't right for Mensch (and I have a very clear idea of what is and isn't right), I always try to say no within 24 hours.

I set up the company from home, so there were few office costs, and made an initial personal investment of £10,000. The website, built by Terry Clark in Mallorca and designed by Adrian Downie, cost about £2000 and then I had to put money into the first book – £1000 on editing, another £250 on the cover design, £3000 on publicity. Of course, begging favours from friends is part of publishing and fortunately I'd been around long enough to call in a few. My old friend Roger Law, best known for creating Spitting Image, kindly designed a company logo for free. Bloomsbury agreed to manage

Roger Law's joyful colophon for my new enterprise

my printing and distribution – although I still had to negotiate hard over the terms.

Mensch exemplifies one of the joys of publishing today – the fact that barriers to entry are so much lower. Back at Harrap in the early 1970s, copyediting was taken so seriously largely because typesetting changes were so expensive. It would cost approximately £10 in 1972 (or £100 now) to typeset a single page, and every correction would cost at least £1. This meant that a 200-page book was hugely expensive to produce and corrections had to be kept to a minimum. It was the costs of printing a book that guided the price, and for much of my first decade in publishing we used a rule of thumb – price the book at about five times the cost (now the mark-up is more like seven to ten times the unit cost) of production. Within a company like OUP this could often lead to perverse incentives, with editors placing higher print runs in order to get better margins – a folly which is as common today as it was then.

But as printing became far more efficient and cheaper, this became less of a consideration, and pricing became much more a function of market and consumer expectations. Nor is it just printing costs that are so much lower relatively. Back in the 1970s, distribution (essentially warehouse storage and transport to bookshops) would be at least 10% of costs – and at OUP when I started it was nearer to 20%. Now it is more like 5%, and, of course, when it comes to electronic distribution, costs become lower still.

All of this has led to a vibrant start-up culture. Experienced editors who have built up expertise and contacts in whatever their field, be it law, medicine or literary fiction, can leave established companies and start up their own businesses. A great example of this is CGP, founded by a maths teacher in the 1990s, and which over the last twenty years has become probably the biggest publisher of school textbooks and study guides in the UK.

In truth though, publishing has never been much of a capital-intensive industry. Certainly when compared to the likes of pharmaceuticals, manufacturing or film and television, there has never been the same need for large amounts of upfront investment. Paul Hamlyn started his first business with £350 in the 1950s, which is approximately about the same as £10,000 today, and many of the great publishing businesses were similarly started from scratch, without any significant investment. There are obviously some upfront costs with any new book, principally author advances, editing, marketing and printing, but these are trivial when compared to the likes of developing and testing a new drug treatment or producing a video game.

And so it is perhaps not surprising that over the course of fifty years, I have had relatively little to do with third-party investors of any kind – be they venture capitalist or corporate financiers. When I have done, the encounters have not been especially successful – the team at Goldman Sachs, although very capable, were unable to help us sell off Reed Elsevier's books division. While I was with Current Science and our plans were at their most ambitious, Vitek and I did have meetings with the private investment firm Veronis Suhler about financing some journal acquisitions that we would (of course) intend to grow and then sell onto another publisher. Venonis Suhler were certainly interested, but it was apparent that the cut they demanded from this would be so large as to make it worthless. This is invariably the way with financiers.

More often, it has tended to be the other way round: publishing has been used to enable investment. Pergamon was a particular example of this – a tremendous generator of income which could then be put to other uses. The reliable earnings from academic textbook and journal publishing allowed Maxwell to speculate, to undertake more risky investments and to acquire companies in other sectors. Later still, it would help to fund an extravagant lifestyle and the purchase of grand properties, newspapers, football clubs and yachts which would ultimately prove to be his downfall. By the end, Maxwell was resorting to wild gambles, insurmountable debt and dubious financial practices, but originally, and fundamentally, his commercial acquisitions and media empire had all been funded by the solid earnings of publishing.

PUBLICITY AND SALES IN A DIGITAL WORLD

Of course, entering a market is one thing – doing so at any kind of scale is quite another, and a feature of a modern publishing is how much is spent on reaching out to the market rather than relying on bookshop displays. For a small publisher such as Mensch it takes up a large amount of the business cost and management time. It used to be the case that a principal job of the publisher was to sell books into shops, and so sales reps provided a crucial role that required commensurate amounts spent on them. But the truth is that bookshops are unable to support the vast number of new books as before and authors no longer make their names and build up their readership through bookshops. Although there are still thriving bookstores, thank goodness, in general there isn't the same culture of browsing among bookshelves in order to discover something – the internet can do that from home.

This is partly to do with the rise of chains and supermarkets – no one would think to ask a cashier at Sainsbury's for advice on what books to take on holiday. But another factor is that there are so many more books coming onto the market – even the most dedicated bookseller, and there are still lots of them, will struggle to keep on top of a week's new releases.

It's not just booksellers whose role as curators and key shapers of consumer choices have diminished. The importance of book reviews has declined with time. Perhaps their importance was always exaggerated, but in the past reviewers had always been a big part of the publishing landscape and the literary critics and editors at national newspapers were significant industry figures, who would be instrumental in shaping opinion and drawing attention to new talent. It was partly the job of editors and publicists to cultivate these relationships and to battle to get new releases into the books pages of newspapers and magazines. A lot of time and effort still goes into sending out copies to reviewers, but it is a frustrating business – more titles are published, but newspapers' review pages are forever contracting. *The Daily Telegraph* used to have a highly regarded team of literary critics and substantial review section – it is now barely more than a page in the Saturday edition, covering just a handful of the week's most high-profile releases. Even more frustratingly, positive reviews don't actually seem to make much of an impact. It is a common experience for an editor to spend Sunday afternoon basking in the glowing reviews for their release in the weekend papers, only to see a dribble of sales come in over the following week.

Book launches and parties also have little impact. I think publishers always knew that, but for much of the 1990s it didn't stop them and the publicists of the time were highly skilled party organisers. While I was at Reed, Piers Russell-Cobb was director of publicity at Heinemann and, among his many talents, was his ability to throw a top-quality literary party and secure an excellent champagne sponsor. But however enjoyable these were, and while also being good for corporate bonding and industry networking, they didn't sell many books. If you were lucky or if there was a high-profile row, you might get a piece in an *Evening Standard* column, and that was about it.

So what does make the difference to book sales? After all these years, it's still maddeningly difficult to tell and in the end, a lot of it just seems to come down (depending on your view) to either serendipity or the dark arts of publicity geniuses. With Mensch's second book, *Getting Old: Deal with It* by octogenarian fitness coach Lee Janogly, we arranged publicity interviews and got plenty of reviews, but it was only when Bel Mooney, the *Daily Mail*'s Agony Aunt, came across the book and mentioned it in her column that it raced to the top 10 in Amazon's charts, and has sold steadily ever since. About this time, we also published *Three Circles into One*, an essay on British foreign relations after Brexit by William Waldegrave. He was interviewed about it on the BBC's flagship current affairs programme *Newsnight*, but this is broadcast quite late at night and had relatively low audience numbers. It was only during the extensive social media activity (and arguments) the following morning that sales started to pick up, with the result that we sold a thousand copies in a week. Similarly, when Piers Morgan unexpectedly sent a tweet commending *Dear Mum and Dad* (an anthology of letters sent from the front during WWI), we sold five hundred copies in a single day.

What makes it more complicated is that publicity should obviously be about generating sales, but there is no doubt that it is also partly a matter of author care – a way of keeping the author happy and making them feel as if their book is getting the attention it deserves. The two objectives do not always coincide. An author still wants a lavish launch party, to be reviewed in *The Times Literary Supplement* and interviewed at the Hay Festival, but none of these things might necessarily drive sales as much as a social media campaign or simply getting the book out to well-known readers.

PUBLISHING BY NUMBERS

Even a small publishing company like Mensch is able to access and track up-to-date sales data. No one today would be much surprised by this, but it has taken more than half a century to get there. The International Standard Book Number (ISBN) came into being just a few years before I started out in publishing, replacing the Standard Book Numbering (SBN) which had been invented in 1967. It was truly farsighted. Not only did it facilitate almost every part of the book industry chain but it was one of the only industries in the world to have a global identifying system. Thirty years later it was one of the reasons why Jeff Bezos, when he set up Amazon, decided to start by selling books. And today, it is the mechanism by which China can control the output of its publishing industry, issuing a limited number of ISBNs each year to state-approved companies.

It wasn't until the 1980s that people began to think seriously about data. But tracking information had always been an issue for a company like OUP, which published somewhere in the region of fifty books a week, each with its own ISBN. Every one of these books would have a raft of associated data, or meta-data as we learned to call it. At Pergamon the publishing data had been compiled and stored on our then state-of-the-art microfilm system, but computerization made this far easier and, as publishers became more confident with these systems, they started to want more data attached to a title, such as its library classification or links to marketing.

There was plenty of resistance to this. When I started in publishing, I was unusual in having a degree in Natural Sciences, and at least (in theory) some degree of numeracy and background in analytical reasoning. By contrast, almost all of my colleagues, and not just editorial, were steeped in the humanities. This was more than simply a matter of what they had studied at university, it was a mark of identity – a badge of honour that distinguished publishers from the industrialists and technocrats, who tended to have backgrounds in engineering, maths and finance. Certain editors were almost proud of their poor arithmetic and their lack of accounting knowledge.

For many of this generation, 'publishing by numbers' was a common and derogatory term – freely applied to anyone who prioritised sales forecasts, production costs or budgets above editorial quality. But things started to change in the 1980s and some of the most able publishers, notably Kim Scott Walwyn at OUP, understood that new ways of generating and analysing data could help them to publish more successfully. A key moment was in 1987 when Francis Bennett set up Book Data Ltd, to enrich the existing bibliographic data, which had long been provided by Books in Print and British National Bibliography, both published by Whitaker. Book Data held all of the information on books – formats, release dates, blurb, key word search, markets and much else, as provided by the publishers (OUP was an early supporter), so that the company could generate a general database that could be used by bookshops. After Nielsen acquired Book Data in 2005, this could be consolidated with information generated by the retailers to provide rich data on sales.

Is book publishing now becoming more science than art? Similar observations have been made about the advertising industry, with the fabled creative director being supplanted by the data analyst. What is certainly the case is that publishing has become far more transparent when it comes to sales. Before the advent of digitisation and systematic data collecting, it was actually very difficult to ascertain how well anyone's books were selling. Back in the 1970s Tim Rix, CEO of Longman and one of the great publishers of his time, once told me that the best way to find out how well a competitor's book was doing was to take the author out for lunch who would then proceed to share sales data as evidence of their publisher's hopelessness (low sales) or their own brilliance (high sales). It wasn't even that easy to know the sales of your own books. This meant that one of the great skills of publishers was the ability to lie, or at least exaggerate, with credibility. George Weidenfeld, a legend of British publishing, never let actual figures get in the way of his best-seller claims, and signed up many of 20th century literature's greatest names on this basis. But this is no longer possible – anyone working in publishing can log onto Nielsen BookScan and find out exactly how many copies have been sold and at what price.

In academic publishing, levels of quantitative analysis are at another level altogether and go far beyond anything as straightforward as sales. In the 1960s, the American linguist and proto-information scientists Eugene Garfield founded the Science Citation Index as a way of measuring the propagation of scientific ideas – or what is called the 'impact factor' of a journal. An ingenious entrepreneur, Garfield established a number of publishing businesses off the back of this, including Current Contents which in its first iteration consisted simply of the reproduction of the contents pages from several hundred life sciences journals, so that scientists could flick through a single journal to maintain an overview of what was coming out in their field. The Science Citation Index, now owned by Clarivate, has an indexing database of almost ten thousand significant journals stretching back to 1900. But it is by no means the only such index and altmetrics, alternative measurements of attention and impact, have become almost an industry in itself. Every year it seems as if another method is invented for trying to measure the success of a journal article.

COMING TO TERMS WITH AGENTS

About half of Mensch's authors are represented by literary agents. It would have been nice to write a history of modern publishing without once mentioning agents, but I should moderate this by saying up front that I have had the pleasure of doing business with many, or at least some, honourable and talented agents over the last thirty years. I say thirty years, because for at least the first twenty years of my career, I barely knew they existed. This partly reflects the kind of publishing I was doing, but it is also my sense that the number of literary agents has increased dramatically over the last half century. Back in 1972, I didn't even know that there was such a thing as literary agents. There were authors who wrote, publishers who commissioned, edited, produced and marketed books. There were printers and booksellers. But what then did agents do? For a long time, it was something of a mystery. To some extent it still is.

One of the stranger characteristics of agents is that, despite commercially representing authors and therefore being led by their financial interests, they could be every bit as irrational as the authors themselves. The reasoning and decisions made by agents would often as not be made for personal reasons as they were for financial ones, and they were just as likely to be temperamental and to bear a grudge as their supposedly highly-strung 'talent'.

This was vividly brought home to me when an old colleague from my time at Reed, Charles Pick, became a literary agent. Having published the best-selling author Wilbur Smith for many years at Heinemann, he went on directly to become Wilbur's agent – in fact, in one of his last commissions, he was in the awkward position of signing both sides of the contract, one on behalf of the publisher and the other on behalf of the author. Later, Pick moved Wilbur Smith from Heinemann to Macmillan, only to become aggrieved when he discovered that I was about to become its chief executive. He was so annoyed that he threatened to move Wilbur to another publisher. In fact, nothing of the sort happened. After Charles died Wilbur and I met and we immediately got on. The publishing relationship was a good one and became a friendship.

But agents, like editors and authors, are features of the industry and working with them is part of the job. Back in the early 1980s, OUP wanted to commission a Marxism textbook covering various social, economic and cultural themes. This was in the days when Marxism could still generate sales and we offered a generous £2000 advance for the book. However, the academic author insisted that we negotiate through his agent, Michael Sissons, who already by this stage was a well-known industry figure. I wrote to the author, copying in his agent, to explain that in this particular case, it would be necessary to reduce the advance, as the involvement of an agent would inevitably result in delays and overhead costs. Not surprisingly, Sissons was livid, but we insisted this wasn't negotiable and he accepted the lower fee and, of course, the author suffered from handing over commission to his agent.

It wasn't too long before Sissons got his own back. We had commissioned the novelist Margaret Drabble to edit a new edition of the *Oxford Companion to English Literature*. Producing such a major reference work would be a lengthy undertaking and so, while still in the early stages of its production, I did what I thought was a nice little side-deal, licensing the out-of-print first edition to Paul Hamlyn. But Sissons, who represented Drabble, got wind of this and insisted that it would hurt sales of the future new edition. He managed to create such a row that we reluctantly agreed to halt the arrangement and Paul Hamlyn was gentleman enough to allow me to cancel the licence deal without penalty.

I hadn't spoken with Sissons for some years when in the late 1990s I suddenly got a call from him, and a request for an urgent meeting. It was in the midst of what was a publishing row and also something of a geopolitical storm. HarperCollins (owned then and now by Rupert Murdoch) had signed up Chris Patten to write *East and West*, his account of the handover of Hong Kong from the UK to China from his perspective as the last Governor of the British colony. The Chinese government had long been hostile to Patten and made its displeasure clear to Rupert Murdoch, who at the time was trying to expand his satellite television business into China. HarperCollins cancelled the contract. As Patten's agent, Sissons now desperately wanted Macmillan to take the book on – it was vital, he said, to stand up to Chinese censorship and to defend the principle of free expression, and what's more he had been counting on a six-figure advance. Our previous disputes were quickly forgotten – we happily took the book on, paid the advance and published a book that sold tremendously well, especially across Asia. And from then on Sissons, a board member of the MCC, would take me to Lords for cricket matches. The lesson in business, as in life, is not to let grudges get in the way.

Personal battles (and friendships!) aside, as the years have passed, the importance of agents has grown and their role widened – working with authors, developing rights sales, and generating marketing ideas in addition to their core functions of ensuring proper contractual terms and conditions. Alongside this, literary agents have steadily and significantly increased their commission. By tradition, a barrister's clerk, essentially an agent, would get paid the shilling in every guinea – or 5%. This was the case with most agents when I began in publishing, but it soon rose to 10% and 15% has now become standard. This is a large rise, and pretty significant when compared to other parts of the publishing value chain (printers, distributors etc), whose share has declined. In order to justify this, agents have had to take on more work on behalf of the author – taking on audio and translation rights and, to begin with at least, the digital rights. The more rights are withheld from a publisher the less responsibility remains and the publisher has become more a financer and marketer than an editorial and publishing partner.

PRINT ON DEMAND AND THE CURSE
OF BOOK RETURNS

Half of Mensch books are now print on demand. They don't get distributed in the normal way and don't have a sales force behind them. They won't get stocked widely in bookshops, but people buy them on the basis of publicity and word of mouth.

There is still resistance in some quarters, but many of the arguments against print on demand no longer apply. For a time, people had qualms about design, production values and whether it could match the quality of a traditionally printed book. But this should no longer be a concern – when I hand out copies of Mensch books, some produced via print on demand and others not, even people who have worked in publishing are unable to tell the difference. Of course, in simple production terms, print on demand is more expensive per copy – but not only does it not require the large upfront costs of volume printing, crucially you eliminate many of the costs of storage and transportation. This is especially pertinent when it comes to international distribution. At the moment, to do a simultaneous worldwide release of a book, a publisher would need to allow for at least three months in order to move stock to all of its target markets, but with print on demand it is possible to send the files electronically and get them printed when and where they are required.

In this respect, print on demand helps to tackle one of the great curses of modern publishing – book returns. This had never been an issue in my early years of publishing – books used to be sold 'firm', with the buyer (i.e. the bookshops) not expected to return them unless there was a specific reason, such as a printing error. At the old counter in Harrap's office in Holborn, booksellers would come in and take books away – they would rarely bring any back. But over the course of the 1990s, this started to change.

As the supermarkets and high street chains began to dominate, they made large orders on the basis that they could return unsold stock and, unlike the independent bookshops, they didn't have the same understanding of their market or close oversight of what they were buying and selling. Publishing companies went along with this, over-eager to secure sizable orders whatever the terms – and the consequences have been faintly disastrous. With the principle of the firm sale no longer being applied, books now return frequently in enormous numbers. With inflation, returning booksellers have even been known to make a profit by returning books for a higher price than they ordered them for!

While publishers urgently need to address this problem for commercial reasons, the other driver for action is climate change and the imperative for publishing to reach Net Zero. The current printing and distribution system is unacceptable in terms of its environmental impact. Producing virgin paper from timber is highly energy intensive, and the print industries are thought to represent up to 4% of global energy consumption. Added to this is the vast amount of water required in producing virgin paper, which is estimated to be as much as ten litres per A4 sheet.

For centuries, OUP made its own paper just outside Oxford – this was doubtless inefficient by modern standards, but it was powered by a watermill and the sheets were taken just a short distance to the print works. The importing of paper and outsourcing to printers across the country brought down financial costs while increasing the environmental footprint. Over the last three decades, as more British publishers turned to off-shore printers in Asia, so the carbon emissions associated with producing and transporting books has become many times greater. When returns are added into the mix, it becomes something of an environmental disaster.

In the mid-1990s, on a visit to Australia, I visited Budget Books – a business just outside Melbourne that Reed had acquired from the Ungar family who had founded it. This was a mass market children's book publisher aimed at supermarkets and newsagents. Robert Ungar, the chief executive, showed us round the modern and well-organized offices and then, on my insistence, into their adjoining warehouse. Here I came across gigantic piles of dust-laden science fiction and western paperbacks, mainly dating from the 1950s. Ungar said he'd picked them up cheap from an American remainder dealer and I told him to get rid of them – it wasn't what the business was about and they were taking up space. When I returned a year later, the warehouse had been cleared and they were all gone. However, when I travelled onto New Zealand to visit our Heinemann offices on the same trip, I was aghast to find the same stock was now there. The managing director of Heinemann NZ told me that he had bought them cheap from Budget Books. Exasperated, I observed that these books hadn't been sold by successive publishers in America, they had failed to sell in Australia and now they were failing to sell in

Auckland. This, I told him, surely had to be the end of the food chain. "Ah no," he replied, "you're forgetting the Cook Islands".

Who knows whether they are still circulating around the South Pacific, but it remains the case that a large number of books are printed overseas, brought back to the UK, distributed around the world to sit on shelves or gather dust in warehouses, before being sent back home and finally pulped. Over the decades, the carbon footprint from constantly shifting stock around has been substantial and, for business and environmental reasons, it has to come to an end.

HOW DO YOU VALUE A PUBLISHING COMPANY?

As I write, Bloomsbury has a share price of 430p and a market capitalisation of £350 million, with most recent annual revenues of £185 million and profits of £27m. This all seems very healthy, but how much is the company really worth?

It took me many years in the industry, and some financial training at Harvard Business School, for me to appreciate how malleable the profit declarations of a publishing company can be. In many cases, the revenues and losses of a company's various divisions are partly a reflection of its internal politics. He or she who complains most bitterly and convincingly about allocated central overheads will be more profitable. More usually in very large corporations, however, the most lucrative activities tend to be understated and shifted around so as not to attract the interest of government regulators.

Despite the financial shenanigans, it remains the case that throughout its history, general book publishing has typically been a low profit business. It is also the case that hardly any publishers go bust. What tends to happen is that, before they go under, they get bought – and not necessarily for insignificant sums. Frederick Warne & Co, the not very well managed publisher of children's and natural history books, was teetering on the edge before being bought by Penguin in the early 1980s for several million pounds. The reason for this is that, lurking within its contracts were the works of Beatrix Potter. The value of a publishing company is not necessarily reflected in its P&L or balance sheet. More often it is the intangible assets held in the form of author contracts – harder to evaluate but longer-lasting than the most recent year's profit or dividend.

So how much is Mensch worth? In its most recent year of full accounts, the company had a turnover of around £150,000 and a profit of about £40,000 (before paying me anything). It has a growing list of twenty titles, with associated stock, for all of which there is full term of copyright and world rights in all languages. Most of the books have a small trickle of sales, some sell steadily and any one of them may yet get an unforeseen boost from a news story or social media mention. A film option has recently been taken on one of the titles by a Hollywood producer and it is always possible that, in ten years from now, another book could get picked up for an adaptation. There are also, of course, some liabilities – storage costs for the stock and an administrative system that pays out royalties.

The point is that, for a 'lifestyle business' which I set up in the year I turned 70, it is possible to build a publishing company that could, at least in theory, be sold for two thirds of its annual revenue, or about £100,000. The further point is that businesses like this are really quite difficult to value. Huge amounts of effort are focused on projected book sales and revenues, but all too often publishers don't think hard enough about the value of the intellectual property rights and the contracts with authors.

THE EVER-CHANGING GEOGRAPHY OF LONDON PUBLISHING

Mensch's office is the study of my house in Hackney. The local cafes provide me with coffee and nourishment during the day, and I have all the computing and communications devices I could ever need. Running a business from home is common practice now, and even more so after the Covid pandemic, and not for a moment did I consider taking out an office in the centre of London. This all seems so obvious that it can sometimes be hard to appreciate how much things have changed, or that there was ever a single 'centre' for London publishing. When I started at Harrap, it was the case that if you worked in publishing then you would almost certainly be based in the West End of London, in Bloomsbury or thereabouts – in much the same way that if you worked in newspapers then you would be on Fleet Street. This was partly because it was advantageous to be close to the principal bookshops. But fifty years is a very long time in the property market, and the economic geography of London is very different from 1972. It is certainly hard to imagine a publisher being the main tenant of Michelin House, which now seems to be occupied by financial consultants and fund managers.

While I was at Macmillan, the lease came up at our offices in Eccleston Place, Victoria in 2002 and we made the decision to move to King's Cross. We found some space by the canal on New Wharf Road, which was close to the Nature offices we already owned, and had previously been a factory making cheap jewellery. We bought the freehold for £900k and spent another £3 million to decontaminate and refurbish it to provide a space for up to 200 people. This was far from being a popular move: people were deeply reluctant to leave SW1, while King's Cross was still an area notorious for vice and street crime. The only other publisher in the area, Phaidon, was paying for female employees to get taxis after 7.00pm for the 300-yard journey from their office to the station. Twenty years later, it now looks like the purchase of the Nature offices was one of the best investment decisions Macmillan ever made, with Google, Facebook and much else besides all neighbours.

London doesn't really have one centre for publishing in the way that it did fifty years ago. There is certainly no need to be close to the Charing Cross Road bookshops, and the days of booksellers coming in and out of publishers' offices to make their orders has long gone. But for all that, the Bloomsbury area has retained its importance and it is striking that so many publishing companies are still located just a few doors down from the old offices of Harrap – though I doubt whether the editors spend their lunchtimes drinking in the saloon bar of the Princess Louise and the snooker hall has closed.

One thing that has very much remained the same is London's unique importance to British publishing. It is hard to think of any other industry, even financial services or advertising, that is quite so tightly associated with the capital. Apart from Oxford and Cambridge, which have become internationally recognised centres for academic and educational publishing, there are no rivals to London for general book publishers, despite occasional efforts by the larger groups to plant seeds outside the capital.

This is both problematic and also a reason for the success of British publishing. It is a shame that, however talented a young editor or publisher might be, they will have to come to London in order to progress in the industry – and certainly if they work in trade publishing. On the other hand, it is the high concentration of publishing activities in London, the density of the networks and specialist skills in editorial, production, rights negotiation and much more that makes British publishing such a powerhouse. Despite the revolutions in technology and communications, this remains as much the case now as it was in 1972.

AN INTERNATIONAL PUBLISHER IN A POST-BREXIT WORLD

My career in publishing has almost exactly coincided with the UK's participation in Europe. In January 1972, the very month that I started at Harrap, Prime Minister Edward Heath signed the treaty paving the way for the UK to join the European Economic Community. Forty-nine years later, at the beginning of 2021, the UK officially left the European Union. For much of this time, one way or another, I was a European publisher – whether it was in terms of the owners of the companies themselves British, Dutch, and German), the editors and colleagues I worked alongside, or the principal market and readership for many of the tiles I published. I have attended the Frankfurt Book Fair some fifty times, and always enjoyed its cosmopolitan and multi-cultural values.

Something that often comes up in conversation is whether the UK, and London in particular, is still the global centre for publishing that it once was. The last few years in particular have raised some doubts in my mind. There is one obvious reason for this: the effects of the UK's exit from the European Union are still largely to be felt, but already our industry is all the poorer for the barriers that have been erected between ourselves and the immense creativity, and enormous markets, of continental Europe.

When it comes to publishing, there are some things that warrant particular attention, and considerable concern. First of all, the campaign for Brexit was in large part driven by the desire to clamp down on immigration and to 'escape' from the EU's principle of freedom of movement. Whatever the more liberal proponents of Brexit (and there were some) may have claimed, this has resulted in a more general formalization of racism, 'hostile environment' policies and the absurdity of bribing foreign countries to take in immigrants who have fled to Britain. This is not only inhumane, but a dire betrayal of the country's best values. It was the UK which, when so much of the world lurched into authoritarianism, welcomed my own grandparents from Eastern Europe and allowed them to rebuild their lives. It is a country which in the second half of the twentieth century built a cultural, scientific, commercial, and educationally diverse society of which I am so proud.

For any observer of British publishing during this period, it is especially distressing. A consistent theme since the war is how the ingenuity, energy and entrepreneurial energy of European immigrants have played a key role in transforming and growing the publishing industry. Whether it is scientific journal publishing, art history, or the market for coffee table books, time and again the great innovators have been immigrants. Many of them, such as Paul Hamlyn, Walter and Eva Neurath, Andre Deutsch, Robert Maxwell, Ernest Hecht and many more were the asylum seekers of their day – people who fled oppression and violence and arrived with little except their talents and work ethic. Ending free movement and treating refugees so that it is next to impossible for the Paul Hamlyns of the future to come to this country is as good a way as any to cripple the long-term prospects of British publishing – and many other industries besides.

The other sure-fire way to wreck the future of the publishing lies in the government's ham-fisted efforts to further distance ourselves from the rules and working practices of the rest of the European industry. In desperation to find upsides to Brexit and somehow conjure up benefits from exiting from the world's largest single market, there has been much talk about regulatory divergence. But when it comes to publishing, the most important regulations relate to intellectual property and these must be agreed through trans-national bodies, rather than being subject to the British government's petty distaste for international law.

Richard Charkin in 2022

POST-SCRIPT

REASONS TO BE CHEERFUL, OR WHY 2022 IS BETTER THAN 1972

There is almost nothing in the literary world worse than a self-serving memoir of a publisher. This is particularly the case when the memoir dwells on the 'good old days' when everything and everyone was better. I am sceptical of such mythologising and feel that I've been fortunate to have worked in an industry that has, in general, improved over the last fifty years and will, I believe, continue to improve. I'd like to finish by summarising some of these improvements in no particular order.

PUBLISHING PEOPLE

One of the most significant and positive changes has been in the huge shift (at least in the Anglo-Saxon publishing world) from nearly totally male to well over 50% female in the higher levels of management. This revolution started quite quietly in the 1970s until now, perversely, if one wanted gender equality at executive board level it could only be achieved by replacing women by men.

There is now thankfully little or no bias against LBQT+ employees, or at least none that I have observed for many years. In terms of race, there has also undoubtedly been improvements, but progress is slow and patchy. There has been a significant uptick in the number of businesses set up or managed by Asian entrepreneurs and the Jewish ethnic minority has always played a strong hand in publishing and other media industries but there is relatively little Afro-Caribbean participation so far.

Other apparent inequalities in the industry work force have been less successfully changed. When I started it was absolutely the norm that editors were private school and Oxbridge educated. This has changed but not as much as might be hoped and this applies to both genders. It is a complex and challenging issue, and there is debate about whether there is explicit economic or social prejudice against working-class employees or whether this is a function of choices being made by young people to find work in more lucrative professions.

COMPANIES

The three job interviews at the very beginning of my career were with Hodder & Stoughton, William Collins and George Harrap, all family-owned businesses, and indeed in the first two cases my interview was with one of the family members (Philip Attenborough and Mark Collins both rejected me). Many of the dynasties that made up the industry in 1972 have been swept away by mergers, dispersal, or simply fatigue. There are many who regret the consolidation of international publishing into four major groups, and no doubt something has been lost, as long-standing independent publishing houses disappear. (Although it's worth pointing out that two of the four conglomerates, Macmillan and Penguin Random House, are still ultimately owned by families.) But the upside to this is that the scale of these organisations has allowed small publishers to flourish, and benefit from lower over-heads, individual flair and speed of response.

In publishing (be it trade books, scholarly journals or educational textbooks) there is exceptional competition between the top companies – for authors, for readers, for technological innovation, for process improvements. This has led to better service and profitability. It is true that the largest companies have often undertaken insufficient product innovation, but this is usually best done by smaller or start-up enterprises – many of whom are only too happy to sell to the big guys when the time and the price are right.

The technological revolutions in typesetting, editing, and digital distribution make setting up a new publishing business relatively affordable and easy to do – the barriers to entry are low compared to many other industries. Of course, most small publishers end up in trouble but there is usually another company eager for additional turnover or a new angle, and willing to acquire an enterprise for at least the tangible asset value and sometimes more. This is a healthy ecosystem and I see no reason why the creative churn will not continue.

TECHNOLOGY

There were no computers at all at the beginning of my career, and now we could not exist without them. The biggest changes came in the 1990s when computer technology morphed from just handling numbers to handling words and images. Things have moved on apace but I suspect we are only at the beginning of the discovery of new ways of presenting information, finding readers, generating income for authors, and improving internal efficiencies. Whilst print will remain a major element of publishing businesses, growth will come from digital applications.

As the necessity to reduce CO_2 emissions becomes ever clearer so the responsibility of publishers becomes greater. Handling books some twenty times between manufacture and sale, putting them on ships and planes to reach readers in distant countries, piling them high in shops only to see them returned and pulped, will have to change, using distributed printing, print on demand and negotiating tougher retail agreements. These changes will not only benefit the planet it will also enhance the availability of books and publishers' bottom lines.

MARKETPLACE

I have always been conscious of my good fortune to have been born and educated in an English-language environment. This confers an enormous advantage in many walks of life, not least in publishing. Producing books and journals in the lingua franca of the 21st century allows us to reach all corners of the world but we have only just begun to realise this. Many publishers still divide the world by country rather than language and in so doing introduce unnecessary complexity and cost. Territorial rights for English-language books are being eroded and will disappear completely in the not too far future.

As literacy around the world improves and as the size of the world population increases inexorably so will the size of the market for intellectual property. There are still large untapped markets in, for instance, Africa, Latin America, and Asia. There is much left to do to instil the reading habit in children but there are great organisations, mainly charitable foundations and the occasional intelligent government agency, who can and do support literacy for all.

AUTHORS

Has there ever been a better time for authors? The barriers to being published traditionally (via literary agents and established publishing companies) may have become higher but the opportunities through self-publishing, podcasting, and social media in general have allowed a burgeoning of writing and publication. Of course, most books will not generate a living wage but they can all generate value in other ways.

For instance, a scientist wishing to share research results can now reach millions of colleagues worldwide within seconds of original publication. English-language texts can be made available to all high school and university students. Poets can upload their own readings on Substack or similar to build an audience prior to featuring in high-selling anthologies. Children's books can be made available simultaneously in all relevant languages. Authors who write in one of the many thousands of minority languages continue to benefit as the costs of publication fall and the opportunities for automatic translation become more widespread.

In addition, it is becoming ever clearer that other media (TV, movies, computer games etc) are feeding off authors' creativity. This is becoming a further income stream for those authors with stories to tell or important information to share. Not only does this expand the market, it also lengthens the life of a book.

AND FINALLY...

Not everything that has happened or will happen is for the better. The reduction in support for public libraries is a case in point. Can there ever be a better 'levelling-up' mechanism than learning from a free resource, the library? But, at least in the UK, government support has dwindled, reducing the quality of libraries which in turn reduces their attractiveness for readers and creates a downward and depressing spiral. This downside might be mitigated to some extent by the increase in free information but it feels that we are at risk of losing one of our most important cultural adhesives and drivers of social mobility.

I could point to other downsides such as the erosion of author loyalty, the lack of normal business courtesies, the growing impact of lawyers and their complex contracts, the power of the technology oligopolies, the growing self-censorship phenomenon. But the future of writing, reading and publishing remains secure. There are far more opportunities than threats (although some of the threats, such as that to copyright, are existential). The world of writing is robust and growing, increasingly efficient and beneficial. Almost every book I have worked on in the last fifty years, from *The Anatomy of the Dromedary* to Madonna's *Sex* has in some way contributed to human achievement, knowledge and pleasure. I am certain that publishers embarking on their careers will, in fifty years' time, be able to say the same thing, and that they will have had careers even more interesting and fulfilling than the one I have enjoyed so much.

POST-AMBLE

If you have reached this far I would like to test your patience a little further.

This book has been a pleasure for me. I am Prince Harry to Tom Campbell's J.R.Moehringer. It has been Tom driving the project and turning my absurd (but true!) stories into words on the page.

Many colleagues have been extraordinarily generous in acting as informal referees, making constructive suggestions, stopping me making a fool of myself with memory lapses or plain inaccuracies. These include Francis Bennett, Patrick Brindle, Bob Campbell, Toby Charkin, Nick Clee, Steph Duncan, Adam Hodgkin, Philip Jones, Angus Phillips, Andrew Schuller, Antony Topping and Simon Wratten.

In addition, I'd like to thank all the thousands of colleagues, authors, customers, and suppliers who have made my fifty years in this business so rewarding and so full of warm friendships.

Now, you may notice that this post-amble is not followed by an index. It was the literary agent Giles Gordon, whose memoir had no index, who explained to me that he wanted people to buy the book, rather than simply look for their name in the index. If the name did not appear they would not buy. If the name did appear they would go to the relevant page, read it, and then return it to the bookseller's shelf. Giles was astute and I follow his lead except to say that if you buy the ebook you will be able to search for as many names as you like.

Ingram Content Group UK Ltd.
Milton Keynes UK
UKHW012159290323
419366UK00007B/51